CRAZY FINGERS

Also by Warren W. Vaché, Sr.
THIS HORN FOR HIRE
The Life and Career of Pee Wee Erwin

Claude Hopkins at the piano. Photo courtesy of Frank Driggs Collection.

Warren W. Vaché, Sr.

CRAZY FINGERS

Claude Hopkins' Life in Jazz

Smithsonian Institution Press

Washington and London

Editor: Tom Ireland
Production Editor: Duke Johns
Designer: Alan Carter

Library of Congress Cataloging-in-Publication Data

Hopkins, Claude.
Crazy Fingers: Claude Hopkins' life in jazz / Warren
W. Vaché, Sr.
        p.   cm.
Based on a journal written by Claude Hopkins,
augumented by Warren W. Vaché, Sr.
Includes bibliographical references.
Filmography: p.
Discography: p.
Includes index.
ISBN 1-56098-144-X
1. Hopkins, Claude. 2. Jazz musicians—Biography.
I. Vaché, Warren W., 1914–   . II. Title.
ML417.H79A3 1992
781.65′092—dc20
[B]   91-38047

British Library Cataloguing-in-Publication Data is
available

Manufactured in the United States of America
99 98 97 96 95 94 93 92   5   4   3   2   1

♾ The paper used in this publication meets the
minimum requirements of the American National
Standard for Permanence of Paper for Printed
Library Materials Z39.48-1984

To the memory of my mother

Marion B. Vaché

and my father

George W. Vaché

c

o

n

t

e

n

t

s

Foreword

The heart of this book, as Warren Vaché will quickly inform the reader, is an autobiographical "diary," which Claude Hopkins—jazz pianist, composer, and bandleader—himself prepared. Thus it joins the growing number of autobiographical volumes we now have from jazzmen, books like Count Basie's and Albert Murray's *Good Morning Blues*, Rex Stewart's *Jazz Masters of the Thirties*, Dicky Wells's and Stanley Dance's *The Night People*, Milt Hinton's and David G. Berger's *Bass Line*, Louis Armstrong's *Satchmo: My Life in New Orleans*, and others.

Why Claude Hopkins, you may ask. Well, consider the circumstances and the associations for a moment:

Raised in Washington, D.C., a contemporary of Ellington's, by parents on the staff of Howard University, an institution he himself attended.

A tour of Europe as bandleader with Josephine Baker and the great Sidney Bechet in 1925.

Bolding New York a couple of years later, a city virtually ruled in jazz by Paul Whiteman and Fletcher Henderson, and with a comer present named Duke Ellington.

Recordings for major labels, Columbia in 1932–34 and Decca in 1934–37.

Arrangements, including the outstanding "Mush Mouth," by Jimmy Mundy, while Mundy was doing his early masterpieces for Earl Hines ("Cavernism," "Fat Babes," "Rock and Rye") and before he joined Benny Goodman.

Then arrangements by Fred Norman, who later wrote for Bunny Berigan, the Dorseys, Goodman, Glenn Miller, Gene Krupa, Artie Shaw, et al., and later still singer Diahann Caroll.

A big band treatment of Jelly Roll Morton's "King Porter Stomp" in 1934, when Fletcher Henderson virtually owned swing treatments of that piece—and before almost every band began to play it.

Hopkins's orchestras, whose sidemen included clarinetist Edmond Hall, trumpeter Jabbo Smith, and trombonist Vic Dickenson—those and outstanding but somehow lesser-known players such as alto saxophonist Gene Johnson, trumpeter Ovie Alston, and drummer Pete Jacobs.

Pioneering work for his band in early sound films.

Relief band and house management at the Zanzibar in New York during Ellington's stay in the 1940s.

Then there are the other realities of the musical life, such as Hopkins's doing arrangements for such "sweet" bands as the Phil Spitalney, Tommy Tucker, and Abe Lyman groups during lean times.

And there is perhaps the crowning glory of Hopkins's career, the fine piano solo album *Crazy Fingers*, a statement of his version of eastern U.S. jazz piano almost exactly as it was in the early 1920s, beautifully recorded in 1973 fidelity, and superbly played. It is as if he were giving us his legacy.

If we want to get a full picture of what the musical life in jazz was really like from the 1920s through the 1970s, we ought to give careful attention to that life as Claude Hopkins lived it.

Martin Williams

Acknowledgments

Some of the material contained in this book was published before under the title "Piano Man" as a thirteen-part series in *Jersey Jazz* from May 1974 to June 1975; and as a three-part series in *The Mississippi Rag* as "The Story of Claude Hopkins," February, March, and April 1986.

My thanks to both of these publications, and especially to Leslie Johnson, editor and publisher of *The Mississippi Rag*, for permission to include the material here. My thanks also to those whose advice and suggestions have helped make this a better book, with particular appreciation for the efforts of Flora Chase, Frank Driggs, Claude Hopkins, Jr., Cork O'Keefe, Fred Norman, and Martin Williams.

Introduction

It may be difficult for anyone who has grown up since the late 1940s to appreciate how very popular social dancing was in the United States between the two world wars, because after the second great war, changes in the social and economic structures of the country brought about the closing of the ballrooms, which for several decades were integral to every large city, along with countless hotel rooms once devoted to dance bands and dancers. Shortly after World War I, the spread of dancing as a social pastime was at least partly inspired by the great success of the dance team of Vernon and Irene Castle with their ragtime-oriented ballroom dancing. By the 1920s, almost every town supported an outdoor "dance pavilion" or a dancehall, and dance bands by the hundreds were organized to play in them. Touring "road bands" often traveled circuits of fifty or more miles over primitive roads in all kinds of weather and in automobiles offering few of the comforts and safety features we take for granted today. In the larger cities, the small dancehalls were replaced by ornate and palatial ballrooms, the bands grew larger, and by the mid-1920s the pattern was well established.

Everything those bands played was designed to attract and please dancers—the melodies, the tempos, the rhythms, the harmonies—and the merits of a band depended almost entirely on whether or not people wanted to dance to its music. Of course, appearance, showmanship, a leader with a pleasing personality, and a certain degree of musicianship contributed, but a dance band still had to please the dancers.

During the teens and 1920s, the phonograph and the player piano were important items in home entertainment, and the popular dance bands and entertainers of the time were well represented on the recordings. But popular music in all its modes—sheet music, records, piano rolls—was generally considered to have no lasting worth. A popular song had a life of about six weeks if it was a big hit, and recordings and sheet music, once a song lost its favor, were ignored or thrown away. The idea of reissuing some records as "classics" or reviving a song from an earlier time barely existed in the 1920s and early 1930s.

Radio came into its own in the early 1930s with the introduction of AC-powered amplifiers and dynamic, full-range speakers, and that made wind-up acoustic phonographs sound tinny and weak in comparison. Soon, phonographs were relegated to attics and cellars, and player pianos became furniture. Many record companies and piano manufacturers were unable to survive the twin catastrophies of the new popularity of radio and the Great Depression, which followed the stock market crash of 1929. Radio Corporation of America (RCA) took over the defunct Victor Talking Machine Company, continuing the operation as RCA-Victor. Formerly prestigious labels such as Okeh, Columbia, Brunswick, and Vocalion became the property of the American Record Corporation, which also owned the rights to labels distributed to five-and-ten-cent stores.

The Depression reached its lowest point in 1933, and many people considered themselves lucky if they ate regularly and had a roof over their heads. Entertainment for many meant an occasional movie, but primarily it meant radio, which had broadcast the dance bands since the days of the early crystal sets. With the development of better receivers, remote broadcasts from hotels, ballrooms, and night spots flourished on late-night radio.

The popularity of social dancing as an entertainment continued during the Depression, and dance bands that had steady jobs and were heard on the air managed to do well in spite of the poor economy. Only the most popular bands continued to make records, and the record industry managed to hang on by catering to a small market.

Aside from organizations like the Isham Jones, Paul Whiteman, and Casa Loma orchestras, the bands were small. The swing era was still in the future in the 1920s and early 1930s. And a dedication to jazz was limited for the most part to the black bands, although some of the lesser-known white bands such as those of Gene Kardos and Joe Haymes played it. The prevailing taste in hotels and clubs was for the "society" orchestras, and units such as Rudy Vallee's Connecticut Yankees and Eddy Duchin's orchestra set the tone. The accent was on melody. Improvisation was almost nonexistent, and brass instruments—usually limited to one or two trumpets and a trombone—were muted.

As the decade of the 1920s began, the best-known bands in Harlem were those of Duke Ellington, Fletcher Henderson, Don Redman, Chick Webb, and Luis Russell. They played the best clubs and halls like the Cotton Club, Connie's Inn, the Savoy Ballroom, and Roseland Ballroom, and they rated quite a bit of airtime. Jimmie Lunceford and Claude Hopkins were yet to be heard from.

With the advent of swing in the mid-1930s, the emphasis shifted to hot rather than sweet, the dance bands grew bigger, and the phonograph, revitalized by new, low-cost electronic developments, returned to public favor. Improvisation by featured soloists became a trademark of the swing bands. Listening to a dance band took on importance equal to dancing to it. And where the saxophones had been the outstanding feature of the sweet bands, the swing outfits leaned heavily to brass.

The life and career of Claude Hopkins covered several decades, starting with the 1920s, continuing through his successful years as a name-band leader in the 1930s, and his later term as a small-group jazz pianist for several decades after. It is well to keep in mind the changing climate in those years, especially the odds against the success of a jazz orchestra in the early days of the Depression.

I first met Claude Hopkins in the early 1970s. I play string bass, and along with Claude and a rather large stable of jazz musicians, I was playing dates booked by Leonard "Red" Balaban and cornetist Ed Polcer under the general heading of Balaban & Cats. The name was a takeoff on Balaban & Katz, one of the most prestigious booking agencies in the days of vaudeville, run by Red's father. A restaurant in East Rutherford, New Jersey, called the Town House served as home base for the Balaban groups until Red found a more permanent home on Manhattan's West 54th Street and got Phyllis Condon's consent to call the place Eddie Condon's, after her late husband's famous jazz club.

Like many people in the New York area who grew up during the Depression years, I remembered many happy hours of listening to the Claude Hopkins Orchestra on radio, broadcasting from the Roseland Ballroom and other locations. I felt honored to find myself sharing bandstands with a man who was for me something of a legend. I knew that

Claude had been working for a number of years as a pianist (I had once heard him at Jimmy Ryan's on West 54th Street in the 1950s), and he seemed to accept the transition from big-name bandleader to sideman pianist with equanimity, but I couldn't help wondering what had brought this change about.

The first evening we played together at the Pines Manor, a well-known night spot and catering house in Edison, New Jersey, I found that working with Claude was easy and enjoyable. His experience of years spent as a band pianist working in rhythm sections was very evident. Today heavy emphasis is given to a pianist's solo ability, and the tendency is to ignore the equally important functions of providing strong chord background and rhythmic support. But this isn't as easy as it sounds, and it requires a natural talent.

Claude had this talent and knew how to accent the beat without getting in the way of the other rhythm instruments. His sense of timing was impeccable. The result was an effortless and exciting swing, never heavy or overbearing, and an adhesive blend in the rhythm section, something always desired but not always achieved.

Claude was a product of the "stride" school of piano playing and had a strong left hand. Trumpeter Doc Cheatham, who worked with Claude for several years at George Wein's Mahogany Hall in Boston, compared his solo style favorably with that of James P. Johnson, who is acknowledged by devotees of stride as the father of the technique.

Off the stand Claude kept to himself, with a sober, almost stony-faced attitude that discouraged personal questions. At least this was the impression I got, and I found out from talking to musicians who had known Claude longer and better than I that it was the general one. What's more, I was told he had the reputation of having a very short temper. I made a point not to break into his privacy and confined my conversations to pleasantries.

We kept working together on Balaban gigs, however, quite often at the Pines Manor, which had developed under Ed Polcer's urging into a one-night-a-week job, and as time went on Claude seemed to loosen up a bit toward me, even to the extent of making small jokes. For a short time we played in a Ground Round location, one of a chain of restaurants, which had the usual sawdust-on-the-floor atmosphere and a basket of peanuts on every table. During intermissions, for lack of anything else to do, we nibbled peanuts until we couldn't stand to look at another one. During a break I went out for a brief walk, and when I came back Claude was sitting at a table in front of the bandstand. At the sight of me he grinned and triumphantly held up a peanut. "I have the answer! Try a peanut with mustard on it."

I finally screwed up enough courage to ask him the question I'd been wanting to ask since we first met. Explaining that I wrote free-lance articles for various jazz publications, I said that I would like to interview him for a write-up. The words were no sooner said than I regretted them. He looked anything but pleased by my request, but instead of turning me down, he told me a story, speaking in a dry, bitter-sounding voice:

"Some years ago a guy wanted to write about me. Said he wanted to write a book. He was a newspaperman, I think. Anyway, I gave him all the stuff I'd accumulated through the years—photographs, newspaper clippings—even loaned him my typewriter and gave him a hundred bucks for expenses. He took off with everything and I never saw him again."

He paused for a second, and for the first time I saw the temper I'd heard so much about. His eyes narrowed to slits, and he bared his teeth as though he was ready to bite something.

"I went looking for the sonofabitch with a gun, and if I'd caught up with 'im I'd have shot 'im!"

"Well," I put in quickly, "I'm not looking to borrow anything, and if you . . ."

"I wrote something for him," he continued, "sort of a diary or a journal. He said he needed it as the basis for the book, but he took off before I ever got around to giving it to him. It's the only thing I have left. I'll bring it along on the next job and you can have it."

He was as good as his word, and the next time we met he handed over the valuable document with no more ceremony than if he were passing on the day's newspaper.

The "journal" he gave me is a homemade affair consisting of unlined paper stapled together, hand printed in blue ink, with sections crossed out, inserts written in the margins or on the reverse sides, and no attempt at embellishment or finesse. There are places where I regret that Claude didn't take the trouble to explain a given situation, but on the whole it's a straightforward account of his years as a bandleader.

My account uses that journal as a base. I have augmented it with interviews with people who knew Claude or worked with him, and with some research in other published sources. I offer it as a tribute to a talented musician and bandleader who has been overlooked.

A Basic Schooling in Jazz

Claude Driskett Hopkins was born in Alexandria, Virginia, on August 24, 1903. His parents, Albert W. Hopkins and Gertrude D. Hopkins, were supervisors of a school for orphan boys in Blue Plains, a suburb of Washington, D.C., just a few miles from Alexandria. They occupied this position until Claude was about ten years old.

Claude grew up to be a good-looking youngster, with a slim, athletic build, a quick intelligence, and many talents. Learning came easy. He was also lucky. His parents received offers to take positions at Howard University, in the northwest section of Washington, D.C., and the family took up residence in the area. His father became university postmaster, and his mother the matron of Clarke Hall, one of the dormitories. For a lad with Claude's proclivities, the move was ideal.

He attended public school in Washington, and then it was only logical that he enroll at Howard University, where he did well at everything he attempted. Besides maintaining a very good academic record, he played basketball, football, baseball, was a member of the track team, and in his own words was "a junior tennis champion." His most outstanding talent was developed in the music conservatory, where he was a superior student, absorbing a thorough grounding in music theory and classical piano.

He graduated from Howard with a B.A. degree, and then to please his father enrolled as a premed student. But right from the start, his heart wasn't in it.

All through school he had worked as a part-time musician, and this had convinced him that he wanted to be a musician for the rest of his life. He felt confident that he had the talent and training to make a successful career in music. His father was just as convinced Claude was making a big mistake. He was willing to concede that music would be a reasonable choice if Claude followed a career in classical music, but, as he viewed it, playing popular music amounted to nothing more than a terrible waste of his excellent training. More to the point, a lifetime of pounding a keyboard in nightclubs could hardly compare to the prestige and respectability of a medical practice.

Basic

Schooling

So Claude—like many a son before and since—did some fast talking and inspired selling to his mother. With her as an ally, he was able to persuade his father to let him take a trial run at a musical career, promising that if he failed to make a success of it in one year he would return to the study of medicine.

By this time he was already a seasoned performer in popular music, learning his craft the hard way—by experience. His first job, early in his college years, had shown the neophyte that in spite of his extensive training he still had a lot to learn. He was invited to join a little combination that was playing in a Chinese cafe at 9th and D Streets in Washington. His fellow musicians were already veterans—two brothers, members of a family vaudeville group that toured as the Musical Millers. Along with their father, mother, sister, and another brother, they had been headliners on the Keith circuit, the most prestigious white vaudeville circuit in the country. In no time it became obvious that Claude, for all his training, was more hindrance than help. He didn't fit in, and they had to let him go.

Claude realized that he needed working experience. For the next few years he knocked about from one club to another, taking any kind of job that was offered, fitting the work in with his school sessions. He joined another trio with Jimmy McGriff on drums and Eddie White on violin. For a while they played at the Dreamland Cafe on 7th Street and then moved on to another club called the Oriental Gardens. Both of these places featured singers who roamed from table to table singing for tips. An empty cigar box was prominently displayed on the piano, where all contributions for the night were deposited. The take was finally split between the musicians and the entertainers.

Claude's apprenticeship in such clubs lasted from 1920 to 1924. "By the time it was finished I finally had a basic schooling in jazz," he wrote. "I had to learn a lot of tunes, and I had to be able to play them in strange keys. Because you couldn't fool those singers. For instance, if a singer asked for 'My Blue Heaven' in B natural, you better not play it in B flat because he had keen ears and would know it right away."

Claude had learned well, and when in the summer of 1925 he had an offer to take a little group to play in Atlantic City, he felt he was ready. Forever after he regarded this as the turning point in his life because it led to events that completely wiped out any further consideration of a medical career. He never regretted it.

▮ ▮▮▮ ▮▮ ▮▮▮ ▮▮ ▮▮▮ ▮▮ ▮▮▮ ▮

The Smile Awhile Cafe

Claude regarded the offer of a playing job in Atlantic City as a real plum because it provided a first-time opportunity to break away from the local confines of Washington and work in the glamorous atmosphere of a famous resort city. This attraction made it fairly easy to recruit a group he called "hometown boys" to play the gig, and he came up with a very respectable little band: Henry Goodwin on trumpet; Daniel Doy, trombone; saxophonist Joe Hayman, and drummer Tommy Miles. They boarded the train for New Jersey with high hopes.

However, as so often is the case, when they got to Atlantic City they immediately discovered the first hitch to the job. The owner of the club, Herndon Daniels, had a friend who played the tuba. Daniels owned a lot of property in the city, and the tuba player, Ernie Hill, worked for him as a paper hanger and general handyman. Apparently Daniels owed Hill a lot of favors, so—like it or not—Daniels installed Hill in the band. Hill didn't play too badly, but what bothered the other musicians was the unusual pay arrangement. Claude was paid for the group of Washington men, and he divided the money equally, but Hill was paid directly by Daniels, and this led the others to suspect that he was getting more money than they were. But they were in no position to argue, so they put up with the situation.

What Daniels was paying Hill proved to be unimportant because he neglected to pay off the right people, and after a couple of months the place was raided by Prohibition agents. The club was closed, and the band was out of a job. What's more, they were broke.

By this time, well into the season, there were no prospects for work in Atlantic City. All the jobs had been filled before the season started. It was a desperate situation, and the band was willing to try anything, so after talking it over they decided to check out a rumor that the rival resort city of Asbury Park, much further north on the Jersey coast, had plenty of clubs and work for musicians. They had no money for train fares, but with the abrupt change in the situation they didn't hesitate to impose on Ernie Hill for the needed transportation. He was the only one who owned an automobile, an old Buick touring car that had seen much better days, but they piled everything into it and headed north.

The trip was an out-and-out gamble. They had no connections in Asbury Park and knew nothing about the place. They weren't even sure they knew where it was, and at one point Hopkins, who insisted on driving, got lost on a back road riddled with potholes. The potholes caused him to lose control of the car and it turned over into a ditch. Luckily, nobody was hurt, and they were able to right the car and continue on their way, but Claude's popularity as a leader was at a low ebb. After the long, bone-crunching ride they were all tired and hungry, and now that they were nearing their destination it was beginning to hit home how slim was any chance of landing a job in a strange town.

When they finally reached Asbury Park, Claude drove up and down the city streets looking for a likely place to stop. He spotted a sign that read "Smile Awhile Cafe" over the door of a small nightclub, pulled over to the curb, and parked the car. Music could be heard coming from inside the club.

"Why are you stopping here?" Henry Goodwin asked gloomily. "From the sound of things they already got a band."

"Well, maybe they're ready to make a change," Claude answered. "Leave all the stuff in the car and let's go in for a drink. I'm thirsty."

"He's thirsty!" repeated Percy Johnson, waiting his turn to get out of the car. "Anybody in this band ever hear of food? I'm starved."

Johnson was the newest member of the band, a drummer brought in to replace Tommy Miles, who quit and went back to Washington after the Atlantic City job folded. Johnson was yet to play a paying gig with the group, and he was becoming outspokenly critical and pessimistic.

"We'll eat later," Claude told him, wondering how far the three dollars in his pocket would go toward feeding the band and what they would do after it was gone.

When they walked into the club there was a five-piece band on the tiny bandstand. It sounded good, but nothing exceptional, and after Claude listened a few minutes he was convinced his group had more to offer. He ordered drinks for the band, and when the owner appeared, Claude introduced himself and asked if they could play a few numbers to show what they could do.

"How did you find out we were auditioning?" the club owner asked, mildly surprised when Claude mentioned they had come from Washington.

"A friend told me," Claude improvised quickly.

"I see. Well, get your instruments ready, and you can take over when this band is finished, which shouldn't be long now."

Claude couldn't believe his good luck. The men wasted no time getting their instruments from the Buick, and as soon as the other band vacated the bandstand, they set up. To a man they knew what an opportunity they were being offered, so they put every ounce of talent they had into their performance.

"How we played because we needed a job!" wrote Claude. "Funds were just about gone, and I kept thinking about what my dad had been telling my mother about this music career. I just had to make it!"

Nobody put more effort into the audition than Claude. It meant more to him than just a job or a means of making a living. It could be the beginning—or the end—of his dream of a musical career. If he had to return to Washington a failure, there was very little likelihood his mother would be able to persuade his father to give him a second chance. Furthermore, his father was sure to make him live up to his promise. If the music idea didn't work out, he would have to go back to studying medicine.

It was very hard for Claude to hide his elation when Dr. Aaron Mosel, one of the partners who owned the club, casually inquired, "When can you fellows start work?"

"Whenever you say," Claude answered.

Mosel nodded, and Claude watched with a sympathetic twinge as the owner took the other bandleader aside and said a few words to him. When he came back, he told Claude he could start working the following night.

"Who is that other bandleader?" Claude asked. "I hope he makes out all right."

"Oh, he will," Mosel replied. "He's local—comes from Red Bank, which isn't too far from here. His name is Bill Basie."

Claude never took the trouble to figure out what the odds must have been against the possibility of his steering the old Buick down the right street in a strange city and walking into what most likely was the only club holding auditions for a new band, but Lady Luck pulled off a near miracle to launch a musical career that day.

As it turned out, the job was good until the Labor Day weekend, when the resort season ended, but Claude was already looking beyond that. Asbury Park isn't too far from New York City, and Manhattan was the next logical move. He devoted every spare minute to writing new arrangements for his band and working up entertaining novelties to add to its sales potential.

Around the end of July a rumor began to circulate in the Asbury Park clubs. The word spread that a wealthy woman connected with Broadway productions was going to audition bands for a tour of Europe. Claude heard the rumor but wrote it off as somebody's fantasy. He was too busy to pay much attention to anything besides his work and determination to establish a successful musical career.

One evening a ripple of excitement and anticipation ran through the club. Mrs. Caroline Dudley Reagan, the woman they had heard about, was there to hear the band. She had dropped in without warning, but thanks to all his hard work, Claude was ready for her. He pulled out all the stops, especially those featuring the band's specialties and novelties. These included a rather impressive tuba solo on "O, Katharina" and his own flashy rendition of "Prince of Wails," which gave him the opportunity to demonstrate his strong left hand. They also played their "pet number," as Claude called it, "St. Louis Blues," which ran ten to fifteen minutes. Claude wrote:

I'll have to explain the routine of this number because it was the cause of getting us the European tour. Our trumpet player, Henry Goodwin, put on an old frock coat, a pair of big, horn-rimmed glasses, a beat-up silk high hat, and white gloves, and with an old, ragged telephone directory he was ready to start preaching in the fashion of an old Baptist preacher.

Everything was done musically. Trombonist Daniel Doy, and Joe Hayman on alto sax, would imitate the sisters of the congregation getting happy and shouting as they do in some of the "Holy Roller" Baptist churches. The bass player represented the deacon of the church, moving in and out of the audience with his battered upright tuba, and money would be dropped in the bell, simulating the collection plate. The drummer and I kept the theme of the "St. Louis Blues" going throughout the entire number. By this time the audience was in stitches, and Mrs. Reagan, who I found out later was a very stern woman, was almost hysterical. I then realized my chances were very good.

The novelty routine convinced Mrs. Reagan that she had found the right band for her needs, and without hearing any other auditions, she signed Claude to a contract. The show she was producing was already into rehearsals in New York, and it was quickly arranged that Claude would start after the Labor Day closing, which was just about a week away. Claude wrote, "Well, there is no need of my telling you how I felt!"

Paris

Immediately after the Smile Awhile Cafe closed, the band made the trip to New York City to take part in two concentrated weeks of rehearsal with the musical show. It had already been rehearsing for some time. A typical variety show, it was comprised of eight chorus girls, a comedian, three novelty acts, a dance team, and the Claude Hopkins Orchestra. It had all the necessary ingredients except one, the all-important key to making it a box-office attraction: a headliner, a star.

During her talent hunt, Mrs. Reagan had approached several name artists with offers, but none was willing to accept the money that was offered. The production had a very limited budget and couldn't afford star-status salaries. But without a headline performer the show was at a standstill, and disturbing rumors were already beginning to circulate that the entire production might be canceled, including the European tour, unless one could be found.

At this critical point, songwriter Spencer Williams, who had an interest in the show, came to the rescue. He suggested to Mrs. Reagan that she take a look at a girl who was dancing in the chorus of the long-running hit show, *Shuffle Along*. He recommended her as an excellent dancer and a fair comedienne. So with nothing to lose by giving her a tryout, the young lady was invited to a rehearsal for an audition. She made a favorable impression even before she did anything. At least she did on Claude Hopkins, who described her as "a very beautiful girl with an outgoing and friendly personality."

She went on to do everything extremely well—singing, dancing, and fitting into the comedy skits without any effort or strain. It was easily apparent to everybody that she had exceptional talent and a commanding stage presence. Mrs. Reagan was enchanted, and with her usual penchant for quick decisions, even though the girl was an unknown, she signed her as the star of the *Revue Nègre*, as the show had been named. Thus was launched the sensational career of Miss Josephine Baker.

Claude collaborated with Spencer Williams on several original songs for the show, and after some more rehearsals—carried to a new level of excitement and accomplishment by the addition of Josephine Baker—the troupe boarded the Cunard liner *Berengaria* on September 21, 1925, for the ocean crossing to Paris. Just before they left the states, the famous New Orleans musician Sidney Bechet joined the reed section of the Hopkins band.

During the voyage they continued to rehearse, and in addition gave two performances for the ship's passengers, one for first class and another for second class. These served as dress rehearsals and helped to smooth out some of the kinks in the production.

"My wife, Mabel, was in the chorus," Claude recalled:

When I married her she couldn't put one foot in front of the other, and didn't know a time step from a sparkplug. But she had a good friend, a childhood chum and playmate, Bea Foote, who turned out to be one of the best singers and dancers in the business. Bea was in our show, and when I mentioned to her that I'd like Mabel to be in it too, so we could be together on the European tour, she offered to teach Mabel to dance. In the beginning Mabel was put in the back line of the chorus, but she worked hard and learned so well that after the two weeks of rehearsal in New York and the week aboard ship, she was moved up front. She was a very pretty girl, and turned out to be a real asset to the show.

Claude didn't elaborate on the ocean crossing or record any private thoughts. If he was aware, for instance, that he was one of the first leaders to take an all-black band on a European tour—preceded only by the famous bandleader Will Marion Cook right after the first world war; and by only a few months, Sam Wooding, who earlier in the year had sailed with the Chocolate Kiddies revue and was still touring—he didn't let the idea impress him. Nor did he touch on a more personal aspect of the trip: his relationship with Josephine Baker. Claude Hopkins, Jr., in his recollections about his father, is more specific:

I've heard all kinds of stories about my father. Back in the twenties when he went to Europe with the show that included Josephine Baker, he and my mother had only been married recently, but during the crossing, while my mother was on one level of the ship he was on another level with Josephine. They were having an affair on the ship. And then he would go back down to the area where my mother was, and they would do what all normal married couples do. At other times he would be back with Josephine. Everybody on board the ship was aware of it, but I don't know if my mother knew, or if she simply ignored it. As it was, that was fifty years before her death, so they were married a little over fifty years.

Claude Sr. had a clear recollection of the other females in the chorus. Besides Mabel and Bea Foote, he listed them in the journal as Evelyn Anderson, Hazel Valentine, Sadie Hopkins (an English girl and no relation), Marion Douglass (daughter of Will Marion Cook), Lydia Jones, Marguerite Ricks, Jap Salmons, and Maria Woods. The novelty dance team was billed as "Mutt and Jeff," and the rest of the troupe consisted of an acrobatic dancer, Tommy Woods; a blues singer, Maud DeForest; a native dancer, Joe Alex; and Louis Douglass, comedian and producer.

When they arrived in Paris the show's cast was quartered in rooms that had been reserved for them by Mrs. Reagan's husband, who was attached to the French embassy, and immediately began rehearsals in preparation for the upcoming opening at the Champs Élysées Theatre. Claude wrote:

We soon learned to stick together wherever we went. In those days not many people spoke English in Paris, and we didn't know any French. As a result, we had to depend on Louis Douglass, Mrs. Reagan, or her secretary, Donald Angus, to interpret for us. If they weren't around we had a hard time being understood. I never ate so much ham and eggs in my life, because that was the only thing I could make those French waiters understand.

The show rehearsed for another two weeks prior to the opening at the theater, and during this time Mrs. Reagan signed a fine French dancer from Martinique as a partner for Josephine Baker. He spoke good English, and he and Claude became good friends, thereby solving some of the language problem. But nothing could prevent the attack of first-night jitters that hit the cast after all the rehearsals were over. They were scheduled to open with a special performance for the press, and the success or failure of the show could well depend on how they went over on that first night. It could mean a long run in Europe or a quick trip back to the States.

As it turned out, they had nothing to worry about. The reviews were all favorable and enthusiastic, paving the way for the *Revue Nègre* to settle in for a nine-month run at the Champs Élysées Theatre. In fact, during this period they attracted so much attention and excellent publicity that they began to get offers to make outside appearances in nightclubs. One such offer came from the Moulin Rouge, in Montmartre, which was owned and operated by two wealthy brothers, Oscar and Ralph Mouvet. It was too good to turn down, and the entire Hopkins band with Josephine Baker gave a performance there after the nightly show at the Champs Élysées Theatre. They shared billing with Gloria Swanson, who was the featured attraction at the club.

When the nine months were up at the Champs Élysées, the show moved on to another Paris theater, L'Étoile. This theater had limited seating, but it was in an exclusive section of the city, so it commanded premium prices.

After ten weeks at L'Étoile, the revue moved to the Cirque Royal, in Brussels, Belgium, which proved to be everything the name implied—a huge circus, complete with animal acts, aerialists, clowns, magicians, and tightrope walkers. The *Revue Nègre* was the last of eight or ten acts, closing the show, and after a short intermission the whole thing started all over again, for at least three shows nightly. Fortunately for the revue's stamina, the engagement only lasted six weeks. One evening the cast was flattered and highly honored by the presence of King Albert and the royal family for one performance.

By this time the revue was a well-established success. Bookings were easy to get. It was just as obvious to everyone that Josephine Baker was quickly developing into a major personality. She had everything this required—talent, beauty, and ambition—all enhanced by delightfully scant costumes at a time when nudity was still a novelty. She was the acknowledged hit of the show, getting rave notices everywhere they went, and she had become a tremendous asset. This proved to be a serious problem later, but in the meantime the *Revue Nègre* was riding high.

The next venue on the tour was a theater in Berlin. The schedule was so tight that after the last performance at the Cirque Royal the troupe barely had time to throw everything into suitcases before being rushed to the station, where a train was being held to take them to Berlin.

The troupe had become accustomed to moving about, and as a matter of convenience Mrs. Reagan kept everybody's passport in her possession, not only for safekeeping, but also to facilitate border crossings as the show moved from one country to another. It saved time and avoided unnecessary problems such as having individual passports lost or stolen. So far the system had worked well.

When the train reached the German border, it stopped and was boarded by a cordon of customs officials, who immediately demanded and took possession of the show's passports. Then, instead of accepting the passports as proof that the owners were on board the train, they began calling out names, insisting that each individual appear for comparison with the photo in the passport. This took time and was especially annoying to the show people in view of the hurry-up routine they had to undergo to get on the train.

Things went smoothly enough until the official who was calling out the names came to Sidney Bechet's. Repeated calls were made, but Sidney failed to appear. A search of the train revealed that Sidney wasn't on board. In Claude's words:

The officers made us get off the train. Mrs. Reagan began making phone calls to Brussels, trying to locate Sidney, which consumed two or three hours, and all this time the train was still in the station. In the meantime, Bechet, flying a little "high," got on the wrong train and was on his way back to Paris. When he got there he was immediately arrested for not having a passport. Mrs. Reagan's Paris connections got our train released so we could get started again for Berlin, and Bechet was put on the next train out of Paris for Berlin.

Berlin

The theater in Berlin, the Nelsoni, was in a wealthy part of the city known as Kurfurfrandamm. The *Revue Nègre* settled in for a long run, heralded by a fanfare of excitement and free publicity in the local press, most of which was devoted to Josephine Baker.

In contrast to the rough-and-ready circus atmosphere of the Cirque Royal, the Nelsoni presented still another variation on the offerings of European presentation houses. It doubled as a nightclub. This meant the revue was required to perform only one show an evening. Immediately after a show, the theater seats magically disappeared, a large area was converted into a dance floor, and tables and chairs were set up. Claude and the band played for dancing, and some members of the cast—especially Josephine Baker—worked with it.

This extremely popular format drew a lot of favorable comment in the newspapers. Miss Baker, in particular, elicited enthusiastic reviews, with the inevitable result that the young star began to get a number of tempting offers. She was pleased with all the attention but for quite some time managed to resist the offers. For one thing, she was bound by a tight contract to Mrs. Reagan, but she also realized that she owed the producer and the *Revue Nègre* a heavy debt of gratitude for giving her the big break to get started. She stayed on, and the show continued to draw packed audiences. But then came an offer that changed the entire situation—an invitation to star in the world-famous Folies Bergères in Paris. This was a tremendous opportunity for the young performer because along with star billing it meant a lot more money. This time the temptation was too great to resist, and Josephine went into a long consultation with Mrs. Reagan.

The result was inevitable. As much as Mrs. Reagan regretted losing her star attraction, well aware of what it would mean to the revue, she couldn't bring herself to stand in the way of Miss Baker's obvious destiny as an international superstar and released her from the contract.

It's easy to understand why the rest of the troupe regarded their star's good fortune with a variety of emotions. Nobody resented her big opportunity or doubted that she deserved it, but they didn't need a crystal ball to foresee what would happen to the show after she left. While she would quickly go on to become the toast of Europe, the show's days were numbered. Without the box-office attraction of the Baker personality and the enthusiastic write-ups in the newspapers, it was only a matter of time, and after a few months the show was forced to close. Some of the members of the cast returned to the States, and others drifted to different cities around Europe to try their luck.

For Claude Hopkins the closing brought about one of the most unpleasant experiences of his professional life, one he never forgot. When notice was posted that the show was finished, it seemed providential to Claude that an expatriate American named Miller came forward with an offer for the band to play an engagement at a hotel in Dresden called the Savoy. Even the name had pleasant associations. Under the impression that he had a group of musicians to manage and provide for, he was happy to sign the contract, agreeing to start work at the hotel exactly one week after the *Revue Nègre* closed. But when he began making the rounds to break the good news to his musicians, he came to the terrible realization that he no longer had a band!

Without giving Claude any notice, or without a word to him of their intentions, three of his men—Henry Goodwin, Daniel Doy, and Percy Johnson—had accepted offers of jobs in Paris and promptly took off. That wasn't all. Sidney Bechet, who had worked and lived in Paris before and could speak fluent French, also wasted no time in leaving Berlin for his beloved Paris. That left Claude with a bass player, who was ill to the point of being unable to work, and saxman Joe Hayman.

This was a new and frustrating experience for Claude. More than once he had had a band that was looking for a job, but this was the first time he had a job and no band. It was bad enough to face the usual difficulties of bookings and travel with a band at his back, but to be without a band was to be out of business. In time, of course, he could reorganize, and in the States it would be fairly easy, but the immediate problem was not being able to make good on a signed contract. In Europe this was considered a serious offense and not something passed over lightly. It could even result in a jail term.

In addition to feeling brought down by the desertion of his men, worry about the contract had Claude at his wit's end. "I was frantic!" he wrote. After desperately trying to recruit replacement musicians without success, he was forced to face the reality that he would be unable to make good on the contract and would have to take the consequences. He held an urgent meeting with Mabel and Joe Hayman, which was described in his journal:

"The only thing I can think of left to do," I told them, "is to go to Dresden and try to explain to Mr. Miller what has happened. He knows I signed the contract in good faith and there wasn't any intention on my part not to live up to it, so maybe if I tell him the truth face-to-face, he'll let me off the hook."

Mabel agreed. "It's certainly worth a try," she said. "You'll go with him, won't you, Joe?"

Hayman said he would. "But I don't know what good I'll do."

I told him, "Look, if they decide to lock me up, it will be up to you to report it to Mabel so she can try to raise bail—or whatever you have to do in this country to get somebody out of jail. Besides, I need somebody along who understands German."

"I thought you said Miller is American."

"He is, but he's married to a wealthy German woman and he talks German like a native."

The next morning we took an early train to Dresden, and went right to the Savoy Hotel. I tried to explain the situation to Miller, but any hope I had that he would understand and release me from the contract was wiped out almost immediately. He was furious.

"What the hell do you mean, you can't open!" he shouted. He was a big man, heavy set, with a florid complexion, and looked more like a German prototype than most of the natives. "I have a contract! You signed it!"

"I'm sorry, Mr. Miller," I said, trying to sound calm and reasonable, "but it can't be helped. My men took other work without telling me. When I signed the contract I thought I still had a band."

Miller's wife, a pleasant-looking woman, who didn't understand a word of English, stood nearby with a blank expression on her face. After Miller stopped yelling she asked him a question, and he turned to answer. Only then did she appear concerned, and most likely it was only because her husband was so upset. She even said something to calm him down, but it didn't do any good. He muttered something under his breath and went to stand with his back to us, looking out a window.

"I think I can guess what this is all about," he said, without turning his head. "Somebody has made you a better offer, a job that pays more money. Where is it, in Paris?"

"That's not true!" I answered quickly. "Just stop and think, Mr. Miller. If that is the case, would we be here? Doesn't the very fact that we've come all this way to explain the situation prove to you that we're telling the truth?"

"I know that's what you would like me to think," he came back, "but I'm not buying it. You're here because you know I have a signed contract that I can hold over you so you can't work for anybody else unless I say so."

He turned and began talking to his wife in German, and this time it was a long conversation. I asked Hayman what they were saying, and in a low voice he told me, "He's talking about calling the police and having you arrested."

I was to the point of collapse.

"Mr. Miller, listen to me!" I said loudly to get his attention. "If you listen to reason, I think we can work this thing out. Will you listen to me, please?"

Miller finally stopped talking, and he and his wife turned to look at me.

"Look," I said, talking fast, "if you'll give me just a couple of days and a chance to go to Paris I'll be able to reorganize my band, and we'll come back and play for you. I have all of my musical arrangements. All I need is musicians to play them. My friend Joe and I will contact people we know in Paris, and when they find out we have a good job to offer them, the rest will be easy. All I need—all I'm asking—is a couple of days."

Miller stared at me. "Do you really think I'm that stupid? Do you suppose I don't know that once you get to Paris—once you are out of Germany—I'll never see you again?"

I didn't know what else to say, but then Mrs. Miller asked another question, and Joe Hayman translated.

"She wants to know what you said. Now she's telling him to let you go, but he still wants to call the cops."

The conversation between the Millers droned on and developed into an argument. Hayman knew what they were saying, but all I could do was try to read the expressions on their faces, and nothing I saw made me feel any better.

Finally Miller, obviously just as furious with his wife as he was with me, turned to say, "You can thank my foolish wife for this. She is trusting—too trusting—but she owns this hotel, and she is willing to trust you to do what you say. You can go to Paris and hire musicians." Then, glaring at me, he continued, "But I don't trust you! If you're not back here in two days, ready to start playing, I can promise you two very unpleasant things will happen. First I'll have you arrested, wherever you are; and second, I'll see to it that you can never play anywhere in Europe again. Not anywhere ever again! Do I make myself clear?"

All the way back to Berlin, the two men talked over the horrendous interview and tried to assess their chances of wriggling out of the commitment. In spite of his promises, Claude was far from confident that he could find competent musicians in Paris, but even if he could, there was nothing about the Millers that made him anxious to work for them. All he really wanted was to get as far away from them as possible.

This inclination was strengthened when they got back to Berlin, where Mabel and the dog they had acquired in Germany were waiting. Some discreet inquiries brought out the information that the Millers had a bad reputation. People who knew characterized them as very difficult to work for—hard to please and impossible if antagonized. Claude was advised to leave Berlin as soon as possible.

Since speedy action was required, it was decided that he would go to Paris alone, leaving his personal possessions behind with Mabel, just in case the Millers should change their minds and send the police after him. If this happened, Mabel could claim he intended to return as promised, but if things calmed down she and the dog would follow in a few days.

International Flavor

Back in Paris again Claude felt a lot safer and a lot better, and before long the ominous threat posed by the Millers was forgotten. Mabel and the dog came in from Berlin without any trouble, and from that point on Claude's main concern became that of reorganizing a band and finding work. The men who had deserted him in Berlin were no longer around, even if he had wanted to rehire any of them. Danny Doy had joined a band headed for South America, and Henry Goodwin and Perc Johnson went with another one en route to Switzerland. Feeling as he did about them, it was probably just as well they were gone, and Claude faced up to the fact that another approach to reorganizing was needed.

Joe Hayman was still around and became the first man recruited for Claude's new band, which was organized to take advantage of a job offer for a six-piece unit from Barcelona, Spain, and which turned out to have an interesting and international flavor. With Joe acting as interpreter, Claude made the rounds of the Paris night spots and lined up a French drummer, an English trumpet player, a Swedish bass player, and a French trombonist.

The men played well enough, but communication was something of a problem. Whenever Claude wanted to talk to the band he had to rely on Joe Hayman, who spoke fair French, or the drummer, who spoke fluent Swedish and passable English. Sometimes it took a while for a message to make the rounds, and every now and then something was lost in translation, but with a diligent use of patience they managed.

After a few fast rehearsals, they went to Spain and worked in Barcelona for sixteen weeks. When that job folded they moved on to Lisbon, Portugal, for another eight weeks, and then to Genoa, Italy, where they managed to hang on for three months.

After a while Claude's French and Spanish improved as a matter of necessity and constant practice, so the communication problem diminished. But he never could get accustomed to the strange food or the way it was prepared, and by the time the band had toured a few more countries he'd had enough. To Claude, used to living and traveling in the United States, Europe in the 1920s was one long and continuous string of inconveniences and discomforts.

Regardless of his opinions about life on the European road, he had other ideas about Paris, and after the band tour was over he and Mabel stayed there for several months. They had carefully hoarded their money and were able to take advantage of the many sites and marvels of the great city. They bought perfumes, soaps, and clothing to their hearts' content, until the novelty wore off, and then at last they were ready to go home.

They took the train to Cherbourg and boarded their ship on March 17, 1927, embarking on one of the roughest voyages they had ever experienced. As one of the ship's stewards confided to Claude after it was all over, the storm they ran into was the worst he had seen in forty years of service.

For two miserable days, Claude was unable to leave his bed and could only eat oranges and grapes. At one point, the ship was unable to make any headway against the wind and the waves, and had all it could do to maintain steerageway. For twenty-four hours the sea held them in an iron grip in the middle of the ocean, and they made no forward progress. In the meantime, mountainous waves pounded the ship and swept it from stem to stern. No passengers were allowed on deck, not that many were foolish enough to be so inclined.

Throughout the storm, the crew went about their duties with calm confidence, as though nothing out of the ordinary was taking place, and this attitude imparted itself to the passengers. Many of them were unaware of the seriousness of the storm until it was all over. Even when they looked out of the portholes at the giant waves and felt them crash over the ship, the apparent unconcern of the crew had its desired effect, and nobody panicked.

The crossing took exactly five days, fifteen hours, and thirty-nine minutes, and when the ship finally docked in New York the passengers could hardly wait to disembark. Claude and Mabel went through customs as fast as possible, and then wasted no time in boarding a train for Washington and another visit with Claude's parents. It was good to be home at last.

I III II III II III II III I

The Ginger Snaps of 1928

It wasn't in Claude's nature to stay away from music for long, so after a brief rest he organized a seven-piece unit to play a pleasant little club at 11th and U streets in Washington. The place was called the Club Bohemia, and Claude liked the name well enough to adopt it for the band. They became the Bohemians: Doc Clarke on trumpet; Sandy Williams, trombone; Bernie Addison, guitar; Bob Brown, drums; Hilton Jefferson, alto; and Elmer Williams, tenor.

They worked at the Club Bohemia for the rest of the season and then, with the coming of summer, went back to Asbury Park and the Smile Awhile Cafe, where it had all started. Claude had come full circle. But he was making big plans.

It was no secret in the music business that the key to breaking into the Big Time was to make it in New York City, and the little band at the Smile Awhile Cafe was confident they were good enough to give it a try. So after Labor Day, all but Doc Clarke and Bob Brown made tracks for the big city, youthfully certain they would soon have it eating out of their hands. Claude described what happened this way:

The road to success in New York was very rough. We found out real fast that we couldn't get anywhere as a unit because the inside cliques had everything sewed up nice and tight, and they weren't about to let outsiders take any part of it away from them. So we decided to split up and try things on our own. But in those days, too, there weren't many booking agents—that is, not many that were willing to take a chance on handling unknowns, so if you wanted to work you had to go out and dig for it.

But I hung around, and once in awhile got a gig—in those days this was the term for a single job—but in actuality it meant playing piano for a "house rent party." House rent parties were just that—parties given to raise the rent. The people living in the flat and giving the party sold food and whisky to make money, and you played from about 8 PM until—. Pretty often during the evening there would be fights, and if you got paid at the end of the night you were lucky. Even if you did get paid, though, it was never more than five bucks, and too many times I left a place without seeing a dime. So it wasn't too long before I made up my mind to get out of that routine fast. It was not only risky but unprofitable.

Things improved a bit when a friend of Claude's, vocalist-violinist Bert Howell, opened a little place he called the Rhythm Club, which became a hangout for musicians. The recreation facilities included pool tables and card tables—although gambling wasn't allowed—and since Claude was something of a whiz with a pool cue, he soon made a lot of friends. As a result, once in a while a playing date would come along. Sometimes Bert would book one, sometimes Claude.

It was at the Rhythm Club that Claude made an important contact in pianist Luckey Roberts, already a prominent figure in the music world. Luckey was so much in demand that he couldn't handle all the dates that came his way and often had to send substitutes to handle the jobs. He was an easygoing and generous man, but he wasn't stupid, so he did not send just any unemployed ivory thumper out on a lucrative date. He knew that the wrong man could do more harm than good, and he had a reputation to protect. Therefore he was very careful to screen his men for their personal appearance, drinking habits, and business ethics. The latter item was very important. There was always the chance that an unscrupulous character might try to move in on the job market on his own, and sloppy or drunken deportment could kill a good connection completely and even lead to the loss of others.

Luckey observed Claude for a while before approaching him, but when he did, he passed on a date that was a critical test and one that Claude never forgot. It was a job playing solo piano—mostly classical music—

for background listening at the wedding party of Andrew Mellon's daughter on the Mellon estate in Long Island. It turned out to be one of the most pleasant and lucrative dates Claude had ever played. It paid $250, he received a $200 tip, and at the end of the evening he was presented with six bottles of imported champagne followed by a chauffeured ride home in one of the Mellons' Rolls Royces.

"Luckey had all that society work practically to himself," Claude recalled, "and there was much more of it than he could handle. So after I did a good job for him on the first one he gave me plenty more."

In 1927 there were any number of clubs where music was played, large and small, in New York City, but the local musicians were fiercely protective of their territory and banded together to prevent outsiders from moving in. It took a lot of time and patience for newcomers to work their way in because few musicians could afford to go without working for an extended time, and most didn't have the patience to wait for a break.

Claude's tenacity finally paid off when he made the acquaintance of the son of S. H. Dudley, Jr., a famous comedian of the era, who was rehearsing a variety show in Lafayette Hall. This contact eventually led to Claude's being invited to attend the rehearsals and then subsequent discussions of the show, which revealed that Dudley was interested in having some original music written for the opening. Claude promptly offered to do the job, a contract was drawn up and signed, and just as though such things were every day occurrences, he was back in show business and leading a little band.

The revue was called *The Ginger Snaps of 1928*, an apt title, Claude thought, because bookings for the show proved to be a snap: S. H. Dudley's father was vice president of the influential TOBA (Theater Owners' Booking Association), which operated a chain of theaters booking black performers for black audiences. The circuit began with the Lafayette Theater in New York, moved on to the Pearl or the Gibson in Philadelphia, the Royal in Baltimore, the Richmond in Washington, and so on through Detroit, Chicago, and other big towns. So the *Ginger Snaps of 1928* production went on tour, seemingly assured of a bright future and a long run.

For a while they did very well, even though some of the houses they played were rather small. At first they managed to overcome this disadvantage by giving three shows a day plus two night performances, which enabled them to keep going, but for some reason the downward trend continued, and only a few months later in Louisville, Kentucky, the closing notices were posted on the board. Claude wrote:

By then we were all in a pretty deep hole—didn't even have the trainfare home. So we talked it over and decided to run a dance with a floorshow, and charge admission. We had one thing to our advantage—we didn't have to pay the talent. We didn't do too badly, but we played for one of the roughest crowds I've ever seen. They came to the dance armed for war, so everyone had to be searched at the door and all knives and guns were checked. This didn't stop some of the fights, but most likely it prevented serious injury or worse.

After the show folded, those who could afford it left for home, but most of the cast were stranded. Claude, as always, had been careful with his money and still had a few dollars. He considered staking the others to train fare, but there were so many he couldn't afford it. He shopped around in the used-car lots and finally purchased two decrepit Model T Ford sedans. Then both were loaded with people and luggage for the long trek back to New York. Each passenger had agreed to contribute to the fund for gas, oil, and whatever other incidental expenses were incurred along the way.

"We looked like a gypsy caravan," wrote Claude. "Every inch of available space was utilized, including the runningboards, which were loaded with luggage. In fact, one side was piled so high that the people could only get in or out of the car on the right side."

The two jalopies—with Claude at the wheel of the lead car—managed to get out of Louisville together, but before long the second car got separated somehow and was never seen again. Nor was it long before the old and worn tires on Claude's car began to give up. They had two blowouts in quick succession. Luckily the second one took place near a used-tire shop, a fortuitous circumstance that Claude was too smart to ignore, and he made the most of it. Preparing for the worst, he bought eight used tires and tubes, and in appreciation the dealer threw in a free pump to sweeten the deal. Claude stacked the spares on the roof of the sedan and tied them down with rope.

The blowouts continued with discouraging frequency until Claude figured out what was causing them. The car was so heavily overloaded that the tires were scraping the undersides of the fenders. He ripped off one fender to alleviate the condition, and after a while wound up stripping all of them. This enabled them to make better progress.

Four days later they were in the Pennsylvania hills facing another problem. The poor old Model T, which had enough trouble hauling its tremendous load on level ground, was hopeless on the steep Pennsylvania hills:

Whenever we came to a really steep hill everybody had to get out of the car, and then the men in the party got behind and helped push it up the mountain. Then at the top of the hill everybody got in again and we'd coast

downhill as fast as possible to get a good start on the next hill. Then we'd
repeat the process. All the while the Model T would be huffing and puffing
and steaming like a switch engine pulling a hundred boxcars.

It was hard work and slow progress, but they finally made it to New York, where they unloaded some of the passengers and then continued on to Philadelphia, where the rest got off:

This left only me and Mabel, and we headed for Washington expecting that
tired old heap to fall apart on us at any time. We still hadn't established any
permanent residence of our own, so home meant my Mom and Dad's place. It
took us all of twenty-four hours to get to Washington from Philadelphia, so
you can imagine the condition of that old Model T. But it got us there—just
barely. I parked the thing on the Howard University campus, and the next
day the students had a ball trying to figure out how it got there.

And once there, the poor thing just died. I was never able to get it started
again, so I sold it for $7.50 to Isadore Glaser, the junkman. And that was
just about the final curtain for the "Ginger Snaps of 1928."

Dancing Schools and the Savoy Ballroom

Undaunted, and still as determined as ever to make a success of a musical career, a few months later Claude managed to scrounge a job at a scruffy place in Brooklyn called the Fulton Gardens and organized another band to play there. It was a living for the musicians but a precarious one because the Fulton Gardens was owned and operated by underworld characters who used it as home base, and from time to time it doubled as a battlefield in the war between rival gangs.

"The manager of the place was a pretty nice guy," Claude conceded:

At least he always took the trouble to tip us off whenever a battle was about to start. When he told me, "Claude, get the band in the back room," we knew there was no time to waste and we'd stop right in the middle of whatever we were playing and hustle to the rear. Sometimes we didn't make it a second too soon, because the fireworks had already started.

You have to remember, though, that this was all during the Prohibition era, and a lot of clubs were like that. You got used to it after awhile. Sometimes after a fight we'd go back and play again—other times we'd just go home. Anyway, we worked there for the rest of 1928 and into 1929—in fact, until the place finally closed.

No job, no band, is the unwritten rule, so when the Fulton Gardens folded, Claude accepted an offer to replace the pianist in a band that was playing for a "dancing school" at 8th Avenue and 67th Street in Manhattan. "Dancing school" was the euphemistic term for a dime-a-dance hall where "hostesses" danced with the male customers for the price of a ten-cent ticket, or three tickets for a quarter. Sometimes a flush customer would buy ten or fifteen dollars' worth of tickets, just so he could sit with a girl and enjoy her company for an entire evening. The hostesses got a percentage on all the tickets sold, and those who were pretty—and therefore the most popular—could wind up with a nice salary at the end of the week.

But it was a rough life at best. Like the Fulton Gardens, most dancing schools were operated by the underworld, so the clientele was of a very low order. Fights and killings were not infrequent. When a particularly nasty fight or a murder attracted too much attention in the newspapers, the police would close the place for a while, but eventually it would open again, possibly in a new location. Dime-a-dance establishments were highly profitable to the mobsters, and there were more than a thousand of them scattered throughout the Bronx, Manhattan, and Brooklyn.

Working conditions for the musicians who played in these places were worse, if possible, than at the Fulton Gardens. At the Fulton the band was able to play normal sets, take several breaks during an evening, and program things pretty much as they pleased. No such luxuries were allowed in the dancing school routine. The band was under strict injunction to conform to the established formula of the business. This meant that no number could be longer than one chorus, and even then it had to be for an up-tempo dance like the fast-moving, gliding Peabody. A slow tune was good for only half a chorus. It was all figured out from a strictly business standpoint to produce the biggest profit for the house. The most the holder of a ten-cent ticket could expect to get for his dime was one chorus. It was calculated that a customer had to spend at least six dollars an hour to dance to fox trots, Peabodys, and tangos. Waltzes were even shorter, so they cost more.

The musicians' status was hardly better than that of a machine, and they were treated accordingly. They were there for one purpose, to grind out short dances for the hostesses, and how well they did it wasn't important. If a member of the band had to leave the stand for any reason, the other men had to keep playing without him. And the hours were murderous, because in those days New York had no curfew, so the band played until the manager said they could quit.

Even getting paid was a risky proposition. If the band got fired for any reason and hadn't been paid, the musicians' union was practically helpless to do anything about it because in the majority of cases, the employer was an unidentifiable John Doe. This made it easy for a band to work all week only to find out that they were being let go at the end of it with little hope of getting paid. An unscrupulous manager, as long as he could get replacement bands to keep the music going on an uninterrupted basis, could develop this into a personally profitable scheme by firing a band without notice and pocketing their salaries.

It didn't take Claude long to find out that playing for a dancing school was probably the toughest job in the music business. After only two nights of the punishing routine, his hands were swollen, his fingers bleeding, and his back aching from the long, uninterrupted hours on the bench.

The other men in the band had been working in the spot for quite a while under the leadership of the pianist Claude had replaced, Charlie Skeets. They all depended on the job for a living and were afraid to quit without any prospects of something better. The group included Edmond Hall on alto and clarinet; Bobby Sands on tenor; Eugene Johnson, third alto and clarinet; Elmer Edwards, trumpet; Walter Jones, guitar; Henry Turner, bass; and Pete Jacobs, drums. They were fine musicians, and it was a good band, worthy of much better than the dancing school grind. Once he had settled in, Claude began talking to them about reorganizing as a legitimate dance band and looking for a better job. It seemed pretty obvious there was no future for them where they were.

They were more than willing to go along with Claude's suggestion, but it was necessary to line up a job before they could make a change. Then Joe Ward, a popular nightclub operator and former actor, let it be known that he was opening a new club, the Grotto, under what would eventually become the internationally famous Apollo. Claude took the group for an audition, and they got the job.

The men were elated. It was a big step in the right direction. At least they were out of the dancing school boredom and had escaped the dead end it represented. Neither the club nor the new job lasted long, but it lasted just long enough for the word to spread about Claude's new band and how good it was. One evening as he stepped off the bandstand for an intermission he was called over to a table near the dance floor. Without wasting any words, the gentleman at the table introduced himself as Charlie Buchanan, manager of the prestigious Savoy Ballroom.

"I like your new band," he told the surprised and delighted bandleader. "How would you like to come to work at the Savoy?"

Claude could hardly believe what he was hearing. This was the big break he'd been looking for since the fall of 1927. After all the striving, false starts, and disappointments, here it was, almost without effort!

The Savoy Ballroom, a Harlem landmark, was recognized as one of the top locations in New York City. Only the best bands played there. Most important of all, it was serviced by a national radio hookup, which meant that the bands were heard all over the country. So what Claude was being offered meant much more than just a good job. This was a priceless opportunity to build a name and a nationwide reputation. It was an open door to the promised land known to all members of the entertainment world by the nebulous title of the Big Time.

Once the initial contact was made, things moved along quickly. A further meeting with Buchanan and Moe Gale, who owned the Savoy, resulted in a contract for Claude, along with the suggestion that he augment his band to a size more suitable for the ballroom. So he added two trumpets—Sylvester Lewis and Ovie Alston—and a trombonist, Nelson Hurd. After some intensive woodshedding to break in the new men, the band opened at the Savoy just one week later.

By the time opening night rolled around, Claude was almost a nervous wreck. Quick on the heels of elation at the offer to play the famous ballroom came the jitters and tension attendant to the fear that his band wasn't good enough for the job—or even more likely, that the sophisticated Savoy customers might not like it. The first night was critical, and it could make or break the band's future. Claude commented:

I had always had soft, melodious bands. I kept the rhythm swinging, but I kept the brass under wraps, and I arranged this one the same way. The only difference between the Savoy band and all of the others was that it was bigger. But I still kept the volume down, even though I knew that most of the bands that played the place worked with everything wide open. I figured we had to be different, yet at the same time I wasn't sure the audience would go for what we were doing. Believe me, it was a strange feeling. I was about to embark on something I had always wanted, and at the same time I was wishing I was a million miles away.

In spite of all the trepidation, Claude was thrilled to sit at the piano that first night and watch people nodding their heads in obvious approval while the dancers crowded the floor. Everyone seemed happy and pleased, the compliments were liberal, and from all indications the opening was a success. Claude relaxed.

The next day, Charlie Buchanan drew him aside.

"Look, Claude," he said seriously, "you've got a nice band and I like it. It sounds good, I'll admit, but I'm not sure it's suited to the Savoy. I can understand that in small clubs it probably fills the bill just fine, but this is a big ballroom and the bands that play here have to play wide open. It's what the crowds here have come to expect, what they've grown used to, and what they want. If you want to make it here, you're going to have to play louder. Let those horns open up and blast."

Claude listened politely but was already shaking his head before the manager was through talking. His chin had the familiar stubborn tilt that was becoming his trademark.

"I'm sorry, Mr. Buchanan," he replied. "I'd like to go along with your suggestion—I know you are making it in my behalf—but in this instance we're talking about band styling and arranging, and I think I've had enough experience in that direction to know what I'm doing. If we play like all the other bands that've played here, then we'll wind up sounding just like all the other bands that have played here. We're trying to sound different—more original."

Buchanan, somewhat taken aback, thought it over for a couple of minutes and then reluctantly conceded. "Well, all right, maybe you're right. We'll give it a try for a week or so." Then he added in a firmer tone: "But understand this—if business starts falling off, you better make up your mind to open those horns, or start looking for another job."

Roseland

Buchanan kept a close eye on the situation, as he had promised, but the next week passed without any problems or complaints, and without any fall-off in the Savoy's business. The dancers continued to crowd the floor as readily as they had when every other band played at the ballroom. But the most convincing argument in Claude's favor was the wealth of fan mail in response to the radio broadcasts, all of it expressing enthusiastic approval of the soft, swinging, Hopkins music.

Claude's approach was basic and, as it turned out, ideally suited to radio and the listening audience of the times. He emphasized rhythm that was never heavy, but had an infectious lilt that invited toe-tapping. The accent was always on the melody, with the saxes blending in a sliding, sensuous mode that was almost a croon. He kept the brass at a subdued level, too. Even the solos were muted, especially those of Ovie Alston, although Sylvester Lewis is to be heard in a fiery chorus on "King Porter Stomp," which the band recorded for Decca in 1934.

In *The Swing Era*, Gunther Schuller, judging the band by records and developments that came along in the last half of the 1930s, criticized the Hopkins style as "at once too eclectic in . . . repertory and redundant in

. . . style." To some extent the judgment may be true of the band later in the decade, but certainly not in 1930.

In spite of Buchanan's doubts, the message was clear—the Hopkins approach was an instant hit, not only with the dancers at the Savoy, but even more so with the thousands of radio listeners. Overwhelming approval resulted not only in the band's staying on at the Savoy, but also in their becoming one of the "house" bands, one of the lucky groups that could count on the coveted advantage of using the ballroom as home base. They worked steadily through 1930 and into 1931, acquiring an enviable reputation. Under Claude's careful tutelage and guidance, the band developed a well-balanced musical character. The men listened to each other, constantly working toward better blending in the sections, and the reeds as well as the brass made a special effort to control their vibratos for sectional and tonal shadings. The overall result was a sound that, along with the distinctive piano of leader Hopkins, made the band readily recognizable. This was especially true on radio broadcasts.

In his liner notes to *Big Bands Uptown*, volume 1 (1931– 1943) (Decca DL 79242), Stanley Dance writes: "Although the Hopkins band was thus clearly well liked and well established, it has largely been ignored in jazz histories. Its distinctive character, reflecting the leader's approach to the piano, was light and relatively delicate, but it swung infectiously, thanks in no small measure to the rhythm section in which drummer Pete Jacobs played a major part."

George Simon put it this way in his book *The Big Bands*: "Claude Hopkins . . . had become well established by the time the big band boom began. His band played a very light, dainty, harnessed kind of swing, highlighted by the solos of Hopkins."

In his liner notes for the 1973 Chiaroscuro solo piano album, *Crazy Fingers*, which reestablished Claude Hopkins as a major keyboard talent, Stanley Dance has further comments on the Hopkins style and the lack of recognition thereof:

There is something decidedly strange about the general ignorance of Hopkins's important place in jazz history.
Back in the early '30s, when John Hammond began writing for *The Gramophone* in England, he referred to an occasion at a Harlem ballroom where the Casa Loma band encountered and was embarrassingly outswung by Hopkins. Previously, the importance of playing "hot" had been recognized, but now the significance of swinging—many years before the Swing era—was increasingly appreciated. . . .
He was never very lucky with his records and their promotion. . . . Besides the leader's delightfully individual piano style, the Hopkins band was always worth hearing. . . . The band, moreover, had a distinctive character, which Hopkins deliberately maintained for a long time. Trom-

bonist Sandy Williams has recalled that, when he played with him as early as 1927 in Atlantic City, Hopkins was already emphasizing softness in the presentation of his music. After the band was enlarged, cup-muted brass became one of its identifying characteristics, and Hopkins remembers that when he first went into the Savoy ballroom he was urged to drop the mutes in favor of open brass. Quite typically, he refused.

Without any question, the Hopkins style—regardless of how critics would view it in later years—was perfectly suited to the musical audience of the early 1930s. In fact, while retaining the soft, melodic approach that was heavily in favor at the time, the band was very much ahead of many of its contemporaries, anticipating the swing era by several years.

It was only a matter of time before somebody else took notice of the young and different-sounding band. This time it was Lew Brecker, owner of the most famous ballroom in the world, Roseland. Brecker heard a Hopkins radio broadcast and was so impressed that he and his manager, Charlie Burgess, made a special trip uptown to the Savoy to hear the band. They sat through an entire set at a table with Charlie Buchanan and Moe Gale, talking things over, and although the bandleader had no knowledge of the meeting, what they decided was to have a great influence on his and the band's future.

Claude learned about the proceedings the next day. He got a call from Moe Gale to see him in his office, and the Savoy owner gave him a fast briefing on the proposition he had worked out with Lew Brecker. If Claude was willing, the band would go into Roseland on a two-week trial basis, with an option to stay on longer if it went over well with the Roseland dancers.

"So what d'ya think?" Gale asked after outlining the deal. He was smiling and obviously expected Claude to be delighted by the offer. Instead, Claude's answer was definitely on the restrained side.

"Well, it sounds like a wonderful opportunity, Mr. Gale," he said hesitantly, trying to be careful of his choice of words, "and I won't deny that I'm flattered by the offer, but . . . well, we like it here. We're happy here. And the dancers and the radio audience like us. I'm not sure we'd fit in at Roseland."

Gale's smile faded in puzzlement. He was surprised and a little annoyed. He knew the value of the opportunity he was offering, and Claude's lack of appreciation was hard to understand. The thought may have crossed his mind that the bandleader wasn't too bright, but what he failed to recognize at first was that Claude was just plain scared.

Claude was familiar with the setup at Roseland. The band he considered to be the best in the world, Fletcher Henderson's, would be working opposite his, and although it was heady stuff to realize he was being considered in the same class, it was also possible that such tough competition would bury him. And Henderson's band wasn't the only one. He also had to consider the caliber of the traveling bands that played Roseland—Jean Goldkette, Paul Whiteman, Chick Webb—even Ben Bernie, with a swinging group of jazzmen who were seldom heard on records or radio broadcasts the way they played in person.

But the main reason for his hesitation was the Savoy itself. The place had become like home. Claude knew the crowds and what they liked, and many of the patrons were like personal friends. Did it make sense to pass all this up for a gamble, even if it did represent more money in the immediate future and possibly a little more prestige? He decided to his own satisfaction that it didn't, so he thanked the astonished ballroom owner for making the opportunity possible, but told him he wasn't interested.

Gale shook his head unbelievingly. "You're turning it down! Man, do you realize what you're passing up?"

Now it was Claude's turn to be surprised that Gale considered the deal so important. He went on to do his best to explain his reasoning, but before he could finish his long-winded and rambling speech, Gale stopped him with an upraised hand.

"Hold it! I think I'm beginning to understand what's bothering you. You're afraid that if you leave here to play Roseland and for some reason you don't make it down there, that you'll be out of a job altogether. Is that it?"

Claude had to admit he was thinking along those lines, and Gale laughed at him.

"If that's your only problem, stop worrying about it. Take my word, if things don't work out for you there—even though I fully expect they will to a degree you can't even imagine—you can come back here. Okay?"

With nothing to lose, Claude took the advice of a much wiser business head and a short time later moved his band to the Roseland Ballroom. Right from the start, Gale's astuteness was borne out. The soft, shuffling sounds of the Hopkins orchestra seemed to drive the dancers wild, and the band was an instant hit. After only the second night the option was picked up for an indefinite run.

They played Roseland for most of 1932. Later in the year Lew Brecker arranged for the band to be signed by Tommy Rockwell, putting Rockwell-O'Keefe, the influential booking agency, in charge of its destiny. No longer would Claude have to scrape and scramble for jobs. He had become a name.

In the meantime, the Roseland radio wire began to work its magic for the Hopkins crew. In addition to a national hookup over the CBS network three or four times a week, they were heard locally on WOR and WHN almost every day, and sometimes twice a day. The Hopkins theme song, "I Would Do Anything for You," featuring Ovie Alston's hot and happy vocal over the urgently swinging but gentle background, came to typify the band's radio personality to listeners. The song, which has become a standard in the repertory of jazzbands, was a Hopkins original in collaboration with Alex Hill and Bob Williams.

The constant radio exposure was quickly building the band into a hot property, but Claude never let up in his efforts to make it into an even more valuable package. Trumpeter Ovie Alston had turned out to be an excellent jazz vocalist, but Claude wasn't completely satisfied. He felt the band also needed a ballad singer, but it had to be somebody with an original style that would be readily recognized over the air and, at the same time, add another dimension to the band's salability.

With this in mind, he kept looking and auditioning singers, both male and female, but nothing he heard filled the bill until a friend suggested he check out a singer working in a night spot called Pod's and Jerry's, on 133rd Street. The singer's name was Orlando Robeson, and Claude was so impressed by his unusual vocal range that he hired him immediately. Then he sat down to scratch out a few arrangements to back him up on radio broadcasts. After a few rehearsals that seemed to go without a hitch, they put him on the air.

Robeson's high falsetto was the arresting novelty Claude expected it to be and proved to be the added feature he had been looking for. In his book *The Big Bands*, George T. Simon wrote: "The band also featured two popular vocalists. Orlando Robeson, who had a high, thin, yet attractive tenor voice, best known for his version of 'Trees,' and Ovie Alston, a trumpeter, whose breathy, swinging style—sort of a Skinnay Ennis with a beat—huffed and puffed attractively through up-tempoed tunes." In Stanley Dance's *The World of Swing*, Claude is quoted as saying, "Orlando Robeson was doing those falsetto vocals before Jimmie Lunceford got on it, and Bill Kenny of the Ink Spots got it from Orlando, too. It was strange, I admit, strange as a woman singing bass, but it was very popular. I also had Ovie Alston . . . and he had a nice little voice, too."

In a few short months, Robeson was one of the most popular band vocalists in the country, doing ballad specialties on such things as "Trees," "Sylvia," "Smoking My Pipe," and "Marie." The extra dimension had been added to the Hopkins entertainment package, and all at once a flood of flattering offers began to pour into the Rockwell-O'Keefe office for theater engagements, movies, European tours, and one-nighters. It was much more than the band could handle, but there was no longer any doubt about it, "Claude Hopkins and His Orchestra" was a familiar name to thousands of people— especially to those who listened to the radio, and in those days this meant practically everybody.

In 1931 the band made its debut in the movies, appearing in a feature-length film, *Dance Team*, which starred Paul Lucas and Irene Dunn. In 1932 they were featured in a picture offering the talents of the then popular team of Richard Arlen and Nancy Carroll, *Wayward*.

Some of the offers for on-the-road jobs were too good to pass up, so with Lew Brecker's approval, an arrangement was worked out so the band could go on tour for three or four months each year and then return to Roseland. The first tour took place in the fall of 1932, typical of many the band was to make, a swing of colleges and ballrooms through Pennsylvania, down to the southern states, up the East Coast, then over to the Midwest and Canada, back down through New England, and finally back home to Roseland.

Records and Road Tours

In 1932 Claude Hopkins was leading a very popular band, and at a terrible time in the country's history. The Depression was settling in for a long stay, gloom was the prevailing atmosphere of the day, and almost every kind of economic undertaking was slowing to a stop or already dead in the water. One of these was the recording industry, suffering from twin ills—loss of its market to the burgeoning radio networks, and the poor economy. Making records was one thing; selling them was something else. As any old-time record collector will recall with gusto, the five-and-tens and other outlets for distressed merchandise were gold mines for those lucky enough to have a few cents to spend on the hundreds, possibly thousands, of mint-condition records that were dumped on the market for anything they would bring, usually for ten cents a record or less.

Only a small number of the many bands on the radio got to make records, and it's a testimony to the popularity of the Hopkins organization that it was one of them. The first session took place on May 24, 1932, and the very first tune recorded was the Hopkins theme, "I Would Do Anything for You," which so typified the Hopkins style, backed by "Mad Moments," an instrumental arranged by Hopkins. At the same session, the Jimmy Mundy original, "Mush Mouth," which Gunther Schuller contends is far superior to anything else the band did, was waxed, coupled with "How'm I Doin'?" a popular novelty of the day, with an Ovie Alston vocal. All the sides were done in one take.

The next day, the band was back in the studio and cut four more sides: "Three Little Words," "I Would Do Anything for You," "Hopkins Scream," and "Washington Squabble." It's possible these were intended for the American Record Company (ARC) labels syndicated to the five-and-tens, but whatever the intention, they were never released. This is easy to understand in view of the deteriorating record market, and it had absolutely nothing to do with the quality of the Hopkins recordings.

The road tours instigated while the band was at Roseland were very profitable. But any illusions Claude may have had that success would put an end to the many headaches involved in leading a band were soon dissipated. If anything, they were compounded.

Following a date at the auditorium in Roanoke, Virginia, the band was booked to play in Charleston, West Virginia. As befitted the name attraction they had become, the musicians traveled in three luxurious Lincolns, and a specially built Ford truck was used to transport the instruments, uniforms, library, and other equipment. This made life easier for the men, because after playing a date all they had to do was change from the band uniforms into street clothes, pile into the Lincolns, and take off for the next location. It was the responsibility of the truck driver and his assistant to pack the instruments and equipment into the Ford and take them to the next venue. This operation took considerable time, so it wasn't unusual for the truck to show up much later than the musicians.

On this occasion the band pulled into Charleston about 1:30 in the afternoon, checked in at their hotel, and then—secure in the pleasant knowledge that they had plenty of time before playing the dance that night at nine o'clock—relaxed. Claude had a lot of friends in the city, many of them former classmates at Howard, so he spent the afternoon socializing and happily anticipating showing off for them that night.

The afternoon wore away pleasantly until it began to dawn on Claude that the instrument truck was long overdue. Even then he told himself that this wasn't unusual and could easily be explained by a flat tire, a slight detour, or a minor breakdown, so he didn't worry too much until several more hours passed and there was still no sign of the truck. Then he knew for certain that something serious had gone wrong and started to watch the clock and pace the floor. One of the most aggravating aspects of the situation was that there was no way to get in touch with the driver of the truck. If it was on the road, all the band could do was wait for it to show up.

The nine o'clock starting time drew closer. Claude was ready to tear out his hair with anxiety and at a loss about what to do if the truck failed to appear. Everything the band needed to play the date was in the truck. Instead of enjoying an evening of impressing his friends, he was facing a forfeited booking, considerable loss of money for the date, and possibly a penalty for not meeting the contract obligation. Beyond that, a lot of people were going to be just plain disappointed. Worst of all, there was nothing he could do about it.

About an hour before the job was to start, the final and crushing blow arrived in the shape of a telegram from the driver of the truck, reporting major motor trouble. Since the telegram had been sent from a small town over 150 miles away, Claude knew it was highly unlikely that the truck—even if it had been repaired—would arrive on time.

At the last minute, and just about the time Claude was about to succumb to despair, a concerned friend came to the rescue. He alerted the owner of a local music store to the situation and persuaded the dealer to loan instruments to the band. In a frantic rush, the musicians were outfitted. This emergency operation saved the day. Although it took a while for the men to get used to the strange instruments—especially the brass team, which had to struggle with unfamiliar mouthpieces—the band knew the book by heart and didn't miss the loss of the library. So they were able to get through the evening in fair shape and salvage Claude's reputation.

Afterwards the men got back into the Lincolns and drove on to the next town on the tour: Logan, West Virginia. The truck still hadn't caught up with them, so they went into a cafe for something to eat and sat around speculating about what they would do if it failed to show up again. Claude didn't enjoy the discussion. Sure enough, time dragged on and there was no sign of the truck, but just as Claude was about to lose his mind with worry and frustration, it pulled in.

It was a tremendous relief to see their equipment again and to know that the episode of the previous night wouldn't be repeated. As the men flocked around the truck to claim their possessions Claude asked the driver to explain what had happened. The man launched into a long and complicated explanation, claiming he had to go miles out of his way to find a garage that was capable of repairing the engine, and then the job took a long time because the mechanic had to remove the head from the motor.

To Claude, with no mechanical experience, the story sounded plausible, but two policemen who had been helping Claude to locate the truck were standing nearby and listening to the conversation. One of them was an auto mechanic in his spare time. While the driver was still relating his long story, the cop moved over to the hood of the truck, lifted it up, and aimed the beam of his flashlight at the bolts holding the head to the main block of the engine. They were covered with dirt and grease and hadn't been touched.

Coming on top of all the aggravation, worry, and frustration of the past twenty-four hours, this sudden and undeniable proof of the driver's treachery was the final straw. In a move that caught everybody by surprise, Claude grabbed a pistol from the holster of the nearest policeman and turned it on the driver. Luckily, the cop reacted almost as quickly and knocked the gun out of the bandleader's hand. It fell to the ground. In a blind rage, Claude made a dive for it, but the officer covered it with his foot.

"Hold it!" he commanded. "Don't do anything you'll come to regret later! We'll take care of this louse."

In a moment or two Claude's better sense prevailed, and he realized how close he had come to creating real trouble for himself. As it was, his lethal intentions weren't lost on the driver, who was standing by looking scared and completely out of his depth. He was more than willing to answer the questions put to him by the police, admitting to taking a bribe to fake the breakdown and not show up on time for the Charleston date, but claiming he hadn't asked any questions about the reason for the bribe. He said he had only taken the money because he didn't think the band's missing one date was that important.

Claude fired the man and his assistant on the spot and decided it would be best for his own peace of mind if he drove the truck himself for the rest of the tour.

It wasn't until some time later that he found out what was behind it all. The home office had inadvertently created the situation. It had booked the Hopkins band with a promoter who was having some unexplained difficulties. For whatever reason, the dance was boycotted, and only two people showed up. The promoter had signed a contract obligating him to pay half of the band's fee in advance and the other half during intermission, so Claude had been paid. The promoter, furious at losing so much money, tried to take revenge by bribing the truck driver to sabotage the Charleston date.

The band went on to play the Logan job and several more towns without incident. They worked to standing-room-only and turn-away crowds because this was their first tour, and it followed on the heels of a solid year of coast-to-coast radio broadcasts. They were a major attraction wherever they went.

Gradually they made their way into the Deep South, headed toward Florida. They were looking forward to a pleasant stay in the Sunshine State but were due for some disappointments. Claude wrote:

I still have a vivid recollection of that segment of the tour, and not all the memories are happy ones. For example, I'll never forget our first date in Ft. Lauderdale. We had to have two state troopers standing guard on each side of the bandstand to prevent trouble from hoodlums.

At another time we were marooned on Key West in the middle of the storm season. We couldn't get back to the mainland because the only road was deep under water. I made up my mind right then that we'd never play another engagement in that place.

These experiences might have been expected to make Claude and the band a bit cautious, but they unanimously decided to ignore the repeated warnings of native Floridians who told them the trip was too dangerous and drive through the Everglades over the Tamiami Trail. However, they did heed advice to the extent of making the trip in daylight, because they were told the chances of going off the road at night were high.

In comparison to the present improved highway through the Everglades, in those days the Trail was little more than the name implied— still primitive and dangerous. It consisted of a narrow track right through the heart of the swamp, which was alive with alligators, snakes, birds, and insects of every description. Both sides of the road were quagmires, infested with snakes and mosquitoes, and easy to get lost in. Vultures the size of small children sat patiently in the trees, watching and waiting patiently for the carrion that was bound to show up sooner or later, either in the form of fish that the cranes and flamingos dropped from their beaks, or the wildlife that became victims of the cars careening over the Trail. Many snakes of all sizes and varieties were run over as they tried to wriggle their way across the road; and sometimes the vultures became victims themselves as they feasted, waiting too long before taking flight from an oncoming car.

It was a scary and grisly trip but an exciting experience. The band enjoyed it, but they couldn't suppress sighs of relief after it was over. Claude remembered it this way:

As far as we could see in any direction the scene was like one out of a movie about prehistoric times. The only indications that humans traveled that way was the road itself and the frequent signs warning motorists not to stop and not to get out of their cars. In fact, I hate to think of how it would have been if we got a flat tire, or broke down for any reason. I can't help but wonder how the people who built that road managed to do it.

As it was, I think the most important sign we saw was the one they had posted just before we entered the Glades. It read, "Be sure you have filled your gas tank!" There were no gas stations for sixty miles. I don't know what people did if they ran out of gas—or, for that matter, what they did if they had a breakdown of any kind. Just getting out of the car would be risking your life. But we made it all the way without any trouble, and I'm glad we tried it.

They went on to play a successful date in Tampa and then moved up the coast and over to Texas, which was well-known in the danceband business as prime territory. Compared to the adventures and misadventures of Florida, the Texas part of the tour was tame and uneventful, with one exception. Once again, the Hopkins orchestra was called upon to establish a first.

They were booked to play at the University of Texas and thought nothing of it—just another stop on the long tour—until they got there. Immediately upon arrival, Claude was met by an eager young student who introduced himself as "chairman of the Entertainment Committee" and an ardent fan of the band. He quickly took efficient charge of things, seeing to it that the musicians were quartered in various homes in the town, and arranging for Claude to stay with the university's custodian, a highly respected man, who had been at the school for many years.

The booking was for the senior prom, and as Claude learned more about it from the "chairman"—a very wealthy young man from Americus, Georgia—it gradually dawned on the bandleader that the chairman was a committee of one and almost solely responsible for hiring the band. What's more, he had gone out on a limb to do it, confiding to Claude that some of his fellow students had objected to his decision, and if the prom turned out to be a flop he'd never be able to live it down.

"If you do a good job for me," he told the bandleader anxiously, "I'll make it well worth your while."

After playing so many college dates, Claude wasn't especially worried about this one, so he told the nervous committee chairman to simmer down and let him handle it. He was sure the entire evening would follow a routine that seldom varied from college to college, which went something like this: The members of the faculty showed up to the dance early, and while they were there the students were on their best behavior. The dancing was sedate and dignified, with the band serving up large portions of waltzes and popular ballads. This lured the faculty on the dance floor and quieted the fears of the heads of the school who, very likely, had already sized up the seven-man brass team with some nervousness and were expecting to have their heads blown off. After about an hour of this—during which Claude received a number of compliments on his discretion and good taste—the faculty left. This was the signal for the band to take off the wraps and open up, and for the students to let their hair down.

As Claude expected, the senior prom at the University of Texas followed the pattern without the slightest deviation. Once the faculty had performed its duty and left after its token appearance, the band lost no time in winning the students over. The mutes came out, the tempos went up, and the waltzes and ballads gave way to jazz and swing. Before long the happy crowd was passing bottles to the musicians and treating them like visiting royalty.

The evening was a huge success, and after it was over the elated and beaming committee chairman handed Claude an envelope containing a note of appreciation and a tip consisting of four crisp one-hundred-dollar bills. The chairman was delighted at being vindicated in the eyes of his classmates, but he wasn't any more pleased about it than Claude and the band.

The tour wound up after a few more weeks in the South, capped by a week at the Earle Theater in Philadelphia. And then—just before Christmas of 1932—the Claude Hopkins Orchestra was back on the bandstand at Roseland Ballroom.

Records and

Road Tours

▌ ▐▐▐ ▐▐ ▐▐▐ ▐▐ ▐▐▐ ▐▐ ▐▐▐ ▌

North and South

Fred Norman, who joined the Hopkins organization at Roseland in 1933 on second trombone and quickly proved to be a loyal and valuable addition, particularly for his arrangements and novelty vocals, also became Claude's lifelong friend:

I first met Claude around 1932 in Washington. I was still in high school, playing trombone with many of the local bands around town, and I used to go to the Howard Theatre to see all the bands when they came through. I'd go backstage with my little charts—the ones I thought were pretty good—and show them to the leaders, and Claude was the second bandleader to give me a shot at writing stuff for his band.

I wasn't able to join the band as a trombonist at that time, because I was still in school, but I would make my charts and send them up to New York where he was playing in the Roseland, and then I would listen on the radio broadcasts. And every week I would send him a couple—one or two.

Later on I was playing in the ROTC band at Howard University, and we went to New York to play for the Howard-Lincoln football classic. That's Howard University and Lincoln University in Pennsylvania, but they held the game in New York—at the Polo Grounds, I think. After the game was over, Claude invited me to the Roseland to listen to the band. That's the first time I really heard them play something in person. And it was amazing! I didn't realize how wonderful it was, you know?

When I finished high school it was right in the middle of the Depression, so I decided to take off for New York and try to make it up there. Which I did, and Claude wanted to put me on as a second trombonist, but I had to wait out the six-month transfer period. So, you know, he was kind enough to let me continue to do charts for him, and that kept me going.

When they went on the road that summer, he put me on as second trombonist, and I had to write a second trombone book for myself on all the arrangements he already had without parts. But anyway, it was done. I joined the band.

I think I was the youngest cat in the band at the time. The veterans in the band acted as though they thought, "Who is this kid?" and they kind of pushed me around a little bit—you know, grabbing the best seats in the car, little things like that—but Claude would tell them, "Wait a minute. Give this man a chance."

Anyway, I joined the band and made that first trip with them. Oh, we went out as far as Kansas City. We played the northern states and cities too—Chicago, Detroit, Cleveland, and you name them—all one-nighters, you know, and I stayed on with the band and continued to write for it.

He is understandably a bit hazy, considering the many tours he took with the band, about the first one he was on. This took place in the summer of 1934, and was a rather brief swing of the New England states, not the Midwest. Fred was with the band for "six or seven years." It was headed south on another tour when his term came to an unexpected end. He took sick in Richmond and couldn't continue on the tour, which may have been the last one before the band broke up in 1940.

The band didn't go on the road at all in 1933 and well into 1934 because the front office at Roseland didn't want it to be off the air for too long. Its popularity on radio broadcasts meant excellent business at the ballroom box office, and in 1933 this was exceptional and not to be jeopardized in any way. Nevertheless, the ballroom provided a solid base to work from, steady employment when breadlines were the order of the day, excellent radio exposure, and freedom to play a number of outside engagements.

Claude wrote the theme song for a package radio show aired on CBS called "Harlem Serenade." Besides the Hopkins band, it featured the Hall Johnson Choir, the Mills Brothers, and a novelty band known as Dr. Jive and the Original Washboard Serenaders. It was a good show and ran for several weeks as a sustaining program, but when CBS couldn't line up a sponsor it was canceled. Also, although it meant long days and hard work, the band was able to play double dates in theaters, which were very lucrative, and there were recording sessions for Columbia and Brunswick during the year.

Another indication of the band's popularity is that for two years in a row—1933 and 1934—it was chosen to play for the Movie Ball, a glamorous and prestigious affair held at the Waldorf-Astoria, sharing top billing with Guy Lombardo's Royal Canadians and Xavier Cugat's Latin band.

With the coming of summer in 1934, Claude and the band were back on the road, with Fred Norman firmly ensconced in the second trombone chair. This time they headed north instead of south on a swing of the New England states and the circuit controlled by the famous Schribman Brothers, Sy and Charlie. The tour included some of the most famous places in big-band history—Nuttings-on-the-Charles, Wilbur's-on-the-Taunton, Kimball's Starlight Casino, Narragansett Pier, Keith's Theater, Old Orchard Beach, the Riviera, Buzzards Bay, and so on. In quite a few of these places a favorite way of drumming up business was to stage a battle of the bands so the Hopkins crew often found themselves working opposite some of the biggest names in the business—Rudy Vallee, Glen Gray, Guy Lombardo, the Dorseys, Mal Hallett, Isham Jones, and others.

In contrast to the southern tour, which had taken several months, the New England swing only lasted a few weeks and was nowhere near as strenuous or wearing, so when the band returned to Roseland it was almost as though they had never been away. But it still felt good to be home.

As the resident band at Roseland, the Hopkins crew watched as other bands came and went on the opposite bandstand. For a while it was occupied by a new band with a distinctive style that was to become a great commercial success, Shep Fields and his Rippling Rhythm. Others have become dim legends in the history of dancebands—George Haefely and his Canadian Capers, Milt Shaw and the Detroiters, along with high-powered outfits such as Glen Gray and the Casa Loma Orchestra, and Paul Whiteman.

But the one that impressed them most was that of Earl "Fatha" Hines, which had built a formidable reputation at the Grand Terrace Ballroom in Chicago. Long before the Hines aggregation was due, the press agents realized the potential for promotion—the meeting of two popular bands, both with piano-playing leaders—and the advance publicity leaned on it heavily. "The West Meets the East in a Battle of Bands and Pianos!" was the theme of the press releases. Regardless of what created the excitement, the ballroom that night was packed so tight that nobody could move. Both bands played their hearts out, and everybody—patrons and musicians alike—had a ball.

Later in the year another southern tour was arranged, and the first date was at a place in Memphis called the Casino. This location had an unsavory reputation in the business. Even under normal circumstances, a black band touring the South could never be quite sure what to expect, often having to put up with rather unpleasant treatment and nasty incidents. However, this was looked on as merely a fact of the business—one of the risks involved in making a living—and the rough locations had to be included on a tour as well as the good ones.

But there are risks of varying degrees, and it didn't make Claude and his men too happy when they heard, just about a week before they were due to play the Casino, that a well-known bandleader had been attacked and beaten in the place. This meant they could be moving into a very volatile situation, where feelings over the incident might still be running high.

It was a nervous band that mounted the bandstand on that first date, and panic almost took over when some misguided prankster threw a batch of lighted firecrackers into their midst. But a job was a job, and in spite of the constant fear that something ugly was about to happen at any minute, the band settled down to work, and the evening passed without further incident.

They left Memphis with a feeling of great relief, and moved on to the next stop expecting the atmosphere to be a lot more pleasant. If they had known they were heading into one of the most harrowing experiences in the band's history, they might have turned back in a hurry.

They were booked into a nightclub about five miles outside the city limits of Little Rock, Arkansas. The place was small and usually only supported a local six-piece band, so it was reaching beyond itself with the Hopkins crew. They were contracted for a one-nighter for the usual hours of 9 P.M. to 1 A.M., and the promoter did such an excellent job of advertising the date that the club was filled to capacity with people from the surrounding towns of Little Rock, Hot Springs, and their suburbs.

Unlike the job at the Casino, Claude had no forewarning of trouble. During the evening things went along smoothly—so smoothly, in fact, that Claude was enjoying himself and lost track of time. The band manager finally had to remind him they were playing past the contracted time of one o'clock. Even then, looking around and noting how much the crowd seemed to be enjoying the music, Claude decided to play a little longer, so it was close to 1:30 before the band played "Goodnight, Sweetheart" to wind up the evening. By then the patrons, bartenders, and management were all well oiled—in Claude's words, "flying very high."

The band began to pack up. As usual, it didn't take the brass players long to put their instruments in the cases and leave, but the reedmen and the rhythm section always took longer. The clarinets and saxes had to be swabbed out and taken apart before they could be packed, and drummers and bass players are among the last to finish up. So these men were still on the stand as Claude genially terminated a conversation with some well-wishers and started to walk out of the club.

On the way to the door it was necessary to pass in front of the bar, and just as Claude was going by the club owner—a burly individual who had been doubling as a bartender all evening and liberally sampling his own wares—jumped out from behind the bar, blocking the bandleader's way. At the same time Claude felt something hard jab him in the stomach, and looking down to see what it was, realized with a horrified chill that he was looking at a .45 automatic pistol aimed at his midriff.

"Where the hell do you think you're goin'?" the man demanded, with another jab of the pistol.

Claude was speechless with surprise and shock, and for a moment couldn't answer. Then, trying to sound calm and reasonable, he said, "Back to my hotel. We've finished playing."

"Oh, no, you ain't!" was the reply. "Get back on the bandstand!"

Backing away from the weapon, Claude tried to explain that even though the contract only called for the band to play from nine to one, they had played an extra half hour, but the club owner paid no attention.

"Don't talk to me about contracts, you black sonofabitch!" he yelled furiously. "Down here no niggers quit on white folks until they're told. Now get back up there!"

At that point the band manager came over and tried to reason with the owner, but this only provoked the man into turning the .45 in the manager's direction with a curt warning to shut up or risk getting shot too. Claude was thoroughly scared. The club owner was drunk, but he also had a nasty gleam in his bloodshot eyes, and his words signified a deep-rooted racial bigotry. Furthermore, he looked quite capable of using the gun.

Nobody in the crowd offered to help or voiced any objections. They stood around watching, either just hoping that the band would be forced into playing again or, more likely, just as afraid of the gun and the unstable character behind it as Claude. Claude was to find out later that the man had a well-earned reputation for violence.

With no alternative, Claude went back to the bandstand, explained the situation to the bewildered and frightened musicians, and with the saxes, drums, and bass, proceeded to play without a break until 4:30 in the morning. By that time word of the incident had reached the ears of the local sheriff, and he showed up at the club.

When Claude spotted the uniform and the badge, he felt a lot better, and when the sheriff walked over to the bandstand to ask what had happened, he eagerly explained. He was further encouraged when the sheriff listened patiently, nodding his head from time to time as though in perfect understanding and sympathy. But when Claude finished his story, the sheriff merely shook his head regretfully, shrugged his shoulders, and drawled: "Well, it's like this, Mr. Hopkins. If I was you I'd keep on a-playin' until the boss says you can quit, cuz you're dealin' with a very difficult man. Y'see, he's already killed two or three men, and I'd hate to see you get hurt."

With such strange advice coming from a man entrusted with upholding the law, Claude realized the situation was hopeless and no help would be forthcoming. The sheriff was just as afraid of the club owner as everybody else. So the band went back to work, and played and played until just about everybody had gone home, and then they were finally allowed to quit.

The men wound up totally exhausted. They were supposed to play another date in Little Rock that night but were so worn out by the ordeal they couldn't do it. And although the newspapers played the incident up with prominent headlines and stories, nothing was done about it. The band left Arkansas hoping never to see it again.

The tour continued into the Deep South, with another jittery date on the schedule. The band was booked for a rather unusual and important one-nighter at a college in Columbia, South Carolina. They would be setting a precedent as the first black band ever to play there.

Claude remembered it this way:

I won't say we weren't nervous about the Columbia date, because we were. After all, we didn't have any idea of what kind of reception we'd get.

But it all started off well enough. The people in charge of the affair took good care of us, and everything went along smoothly and normally until about the middle of the second set. Then a couple of students who had been nipping at a jug of corn whisky planted themselves in front of the band and began heckling the musicians. They resorted to some pretty vile insults, trying to get a rise out of the men, but I had given strict instructions to ignore them.

So when the kids found out their tactics didn't work, they tried another angle. This time they insisted on offering drinks to the men from the jug. When nobody accepted their offers they picked on poor Fred Norman—who didn't drink under any circumstances—and forced him to swallow about half a glass of the stuff. It immediately made him so sick that he had to be carried out.

And I guess this either satisfied the hecklers or it scared them, because from then on they left us alone. Some of the other students revived Fred, and the rest of the evening was peaceful.

The worst was now behind them, and things took a decided turn for the better when they reached Louisiana. First they played a successful date at the civic auditorium in Baton Rouge, and then they moved on to New Orleans, where the red-carpet treatment awaited them: "New Orleans was a city I had always wanted to visit," wrote Claude, "and we really had a great time there. We were booked to play at the Fair Grounds, and on the day of the dance they held a big parade through the city for us, complete with floats and bands. There were numerous parties and banquets too, and that night a crowd of over 12,000 people came to hear the band."

Claude and the musicians liked New Orleans so much that he called the home office and arranged for the band to have some time off. They settled in for four or five days, visiting the high spots and historical landmarks around the town. When it came time to leave, they hated to go, but they had to start the upswing back to New York.

They worked their way up the Gulf Coast, playing a date in Biloxi, Mississippi—which Claude described as "a beautiful resort"—and then traveled east to Montgomery, Alabama, and then on to Atlanta, Charlotte, and Winston-Salem.

The Winston-Salem job was exceptional for a couple of reasons. For one thing, the band had to play in a huge tobacco warehouse because it was the only location in town big enough to hold the huge crowd they drew; and for another, the dance was promoted by a personal friend of Claude's, E. C. Hill. The event proved to be a sellout, and Hill cleaned up, but so did the band. Besides a $1,000 guarantee, they earned 60 percent of the gate receipts. The $1,000 guarantee alone was more than most bands were getting at the time, and Claude's was among the first to break this barrier and also collect a sizable percentage of the gate, ushering in a new era of prosperity for bandleaders and musicians.

The Cotton Club

From the standpoint of its recording career, 1934 was the peak year for the Hopkins organization, with sessions for Columbia, Brunswick, and Decca. All of the sides were released in this country, and a number of them abroad. No doubt the radio broadcasts from Roseland, which kept the band in front of the public on a regular basis, were largely responsible. But this is one instance where the Hopkins luck didn't hold up. It is easy to extrapolate from what we know of the record market that developed only a short time later that the Hopkins records were a year or two ahead of their time. It's interesting to speculate how they might have been received in the latter part of 1935 or 1936. As it is, the band had only one commercial session for Decca in 1935, early in the year, and none at all in 1936.

However, it's possible that a few recording sessions later in 1935 might have made an amazing difference in the band's future, because there is good reason to believe the band was at its peak at the time it went unrecorded. Fred Norman put it this way: "When we were at Roseland— a little bit before we got the offer to go into the 'Cotton Club'—the band was really cookin'. At night, a little after midnight when all the hotel entertainment rooms had closed, a lot of white musicians used to come over and stand and listen to the cats play."

In November 1934 the Claude Hopkins Orchestra made another auspicious move, one that seemed to open the doors to unlimited opportunity for the band as a unit and push Claude up another notch in the hierarchy of name bandleaders. Lew Brecker, who had already done so much to promote the band, and the Rockwell-O'Keefe agency worked out a deal to book the band into New York's most famous Harlem nightspot, the Cotton Club.

It's easy to understand why Claude was elated. On the face of it, he was being offered a tremendous opportunity. Any band that played the Cotton Club automatically enjoyed great prestige, but it also meant working with some of the finest entertainers in show business. On the bill with the Hopkins orchestra would be Bill "Bojangles" Robinson, the Nicholas Brothers, Rubberlegs Williams, Nina Mae McKinney, Butterbeans and Susie, and Cora LaRedd—all of them headliners. In addition, the floor show featured a chorus line of sixteen talented and attractive girls, backed by eight tall and stately "picture girls," who weren't required to do anything but stand around and look beautiful.

The band would play for dancing, but its primary function was backing the shows. The Cotton Club productions were equal to any theater presentations, with original music, elaborate sets, and top talent—no small challenge to any musical organization.

Claude moved in with his regular band but wisely hired Russell "Pops" Smith, who for many years had been a mainstay with Fletcher Henderson, to play lead trumpet. Other changes also took place at this time, according to Fred Norman: "When we got to the Cotton Club, which was a big move for Claude at the time, the personnel of the band changed a bit. I know Hilton Jefferson joined us on alto sax, and we had a fellow named Henry Wells on trombone with myself. Claude was trying to strengthen the band. . . . Now, that Cotton Club band was something else!"

The show the Hopkins unit was to play for had been rehearsing all summer. Produced by Elida Webb and Leonard Warner, and arranged by Will Vodery, it proved to be well up to Cotton Club standards and played to good audiences. Running time for each performance averaged from an hour and forty-five minutes to two-and-a-half hours, and there were three shows nightly. If business was particularly good, a fourth show was staged, and since attendance was usually excellent, this happened frequently.

The Rockwell-O'Keefe agency had been handling the band since its early days at Roseland, and Claude and Cork O'Keefe became good friends. O'Keefe recalled:

Claude Hopkins was a first-class gentleman. He had a good band, and he played fine piano. We booked Claude's band for a number of years, starting back when he was playing at Roseland, and it was tough going in the early days because, unfortunately, the band didn't reach the commercial value for income it was entitled to musically. But later on one of the things he did that was good for me and for the company was when we had them booked for the Cotton Club. It was a good band; they played well, and Claude played great piano. And, as I've said, he was a real gentleman—a real, high-class, genuine gentleman.

Things were going very well at the Cotton Club, when we were suddenly hit with a demand from the American Federation of Musicians to surrender our booking license. Then in quick order we received a notice from Local 802 saying, "You are hereby accused of so-and-so and so-and-so, and you are to appear for trial on such-and-such a date," and all the rest of the union jargon on the form. I never could prove who was behind all this, but I never doubted it was instigated by MCA [Music Corporation of America]. The competition in the music business was fierce, and MCA never backed away from anything that might be to their advantage. And Sonny Werblin [head of MCA] was one of my closest friends.

The ridiculous charge that somebody had dreamed up was that Rockwell-O'Keefe, entrusted with the payroll for the Cotton Club musicians, was paying those musicians under union scale. If anything was ever untrue, this was it. First of all, you have to realize who we were dealing with. It was common knowledge that you never did anything to get the Cotton Club in trouble or to upset the boys who ran it without taking a chance of never seeing your wife again.

At this late date I don't remember exactly how the payroll was handled, but I don't think we had anything to do with making it up. Maybe we delivered it to the Cotton Club, but I seem to recall this was Mike Nidorf's department, and I never paid much attention to it. Mike worked for us and later became a partner in the firm.

Claude Hopkins and his band were playing the club. It's possible that Mike cashed the Cotton Club check and then brought the money to Claude, and Claude paid the musicians—but what the union was implying was that Claude was underpaying his musicians.

Well, first we got this tough summons to appear before the union trial board, and in the meantime we got a call from the national federation office demanding that we send in our license. My answer to this was, "If you want it, come and get it!"—typical fresh O'Keefe—and I took the thing off the wall and locked it up in the big safe we had in the office. But it looked like we were in a lot of trouble.

Around the same time we were getting these notices, Claude was called into union headquarters to find out what the charges were against him. At that time union headquarters were right across the street. We occupied practically the whole twenty-first floor in the building which also houses Radio City Music Hall. I was asking Mike Nidorf about the charges, which he promptly labeled untrue, when Claude Hopkins walked in. He came over to me and said, "Mr. O'Keefe, it looks like I've got you in for a whole lot of trouble. You, personally."

I said, "I don't know what it's all about, Claude. Do you?"

"There's no truth in it. My men are getting paid union scale and, as you know, I'm working for practically nothing myself just to keep the job. The problem is, I got a trumpet player, named so-and-so, who's a foreigner and doesn't know how things operate around here—and now, as it turns out, he's also a troublemaker."

He went on to tell the story behind the charges. Of course, as everybody knows, one of the biggest attractions at the Cotton Club was the chorus line. You wouldn't see any more beautiful girls anywhere than in those shows they put together, and some of the girls were fine performers. Lena Horne sang and was in the chorus line; Ethel Waters sang at the club. So Claude's trumpet player was greatly taken with one of the beauties, and went on the make for her. Not only was this very poor judgement on his part, it was dangerous. It was an unwritten law in nightclubs like this one that although the musicians could look and admire, they weren't allowed to touch. More often than not, the girls were already spoken for, and by people with very strong voices.

The trumpet player was warned to stay away, but he didn't stop his attentions, and after he ignored several warnings the roof fell in. He went to work one night and was met by some of "the boys." It seems the chorus girl was the lady friend of one of the owners of the club. The boys didn't mince words. There was a rear stairway in the club that led to a back alley. They threw the guy down the stairs and told him to get the hell off the property before he wound up dead, and to stay away from the club.

The next morning our trouble started. The trumpet player went to the union and complained. What he expected to gain, I don't know, or how the charges were made up. But when Claude came to see me, he said, "Mr. O'Keefe, when the trial comes, I want you to know that I, personally, am going to testify that you, Rockwell-O'Keefe, or Mr. Nidorf, were never involved in this thing. I've got all the boys in the band ready to testify that you people were not involved in any way in paying the musicians. You had nothing to do with it." And then he said, "And for all you've done for me—you, personally. . ." He broke off, came over, and put his arms around me.

The trial never did come off. Time dragged on, and somehow after a while we were not in as much trouble with 802 as we had been, because all the while we weren't supposed to have a booking license we were calling Max Ahrons [president of Local 802, New York] and asking, "Have you set the trial date yet?" But nothing happened. Still the people in our office were getting nervous. According to the union rules we weren't supposed to be booking bands. I told them, "Look at all the boys we have depending on us for work. If we don't book the ten or fifteen bands we have that's anywhere from 150 to 200 men that are going to be out of work. What do you suggest we do, give them up and let somebody else book them?"

And then one day the phone rang and it was Bert Henderson again. He was the one who had asked for our booking license, and he was the assistant to Mr. Weber [Josef Weber, president of the American Federation of Musicians], the man who founded the union and was its head man. "Mr. O'Keefe," he said, "the chief wants to know if you'll be available to make an appointment to come over to his office soon?"

We made the appointment for the next day, and it turned out that Weber was more concerned about the proliferation of incorporated bands like Casa Loma than he was about the charges against us. After I had promised not to encourage any more bands to incorporate, he was satisfied.

A short time later we were informed that our license was valid again, so I took it out of the safe and hung it back on the wall. But poor Claude—he had to live with that cloud over his head for some time.

With customary caution, O'Keefe never mentioned the trumpet player's name who created all the trouble at the Cotton Club, and although Fred Norman confirmed the story to the extent that he remembered a musician getting into difficulty, he couldn't recall who it was and tended to doubt it was a trumpet player. The most likely candidate would be the trombonist, Fernando Arbello, a Puerto Rican, who left the band around this time, possibly to be replaced by Vic Dickenson. However, Arbello is listed as still in the band when it recorded a transcription date on October 18, 1935, which resulted in sixteen tracks that have been issued on Jazz Archives JA-27 under the title, *Singin' in the Rain: Claude Hopkins and His Cotton Club Orchestra.*

In his liner notes for this album, Frank Driggs made some very astute and pertinent observations:

The epitome of smooth sensuous swing, that was the Claude Hopkins orchestra of the middle 1930s. Impeccably groomed, tall, handsome, and sophisticated, the leader displayed his abundant keyboard wizardy on nearly everything he played. Claude's success was achieved right behind Duke Ellington's although few of his sidemen matched those of the Ellington or Fletcher Henderson bands for solo achievements. Claude built his band from the rhythm up and always had one of the smoothest in the business. Drummer Pete Jacobs, bassist Henry Turner and guitarist Walter Jones meshed together and gave the band its solid base. They were a team for nearly seven years, and some very fine recordings resulted on the Columbia, Brunswick and Decca labels.

If you, the listener, happened to be of an age at this time in history you might well have journeyed uptown to the Cotton Club where Claude's band was playing for dancing and also backing the fine productions featuring Adelaide Hall, Cora LaRedd and many other fine stars of song and dance. The Cotton Club was on its last legs so far as Harlem was concerned and would move downtown in 1936 and reopen on the site of the old Connie's Inn which had folded earlier in the year. . . .

It was an era of superb looking and sounding musicians and musicianship. It is a time we shall not see again.

pictures. I found out that he was a very shy person, and he always came to the club by himself. He told me his main pleasures were fishing and flying."

Ordinarily the shows at the Cotton Club lasted about nine months, or a year at the most, but this time the production carried on for a full two years. The Hopkins band played the entire period, enjoying national exposure on network radio several times a week. It was generally conceded in those days that any band that played the Cotton Club had reached the peak of musical attainment, and this—along with two solid years of broadcasting—combined to make the band a very hot property, much in demand by promoters.

But the Cotton Club was to be the band's last extended location job, and from that point on they were almost constantly on the road. Fred Norman, looking back at what happened after the Cotton Club period, suggested that cutting ties with Roseland was the mistake that finally led to the band's breakup. During the Roseland years, the band always had a home base to return to after a long road tour, where it could resume broadcasting on a steady basis and renew its popularity with the radio audience throughout the country. From now on, that security would be missing.

Of course, in 1936 this idea never occurred to anybody, and right after the Cotton Club show closed on New Year's Eve, the band hit the road again. This time it was a tour of Canada. As Frank Driggs noted in his liner notes, this was the end of the uptown Harlem location of the Cotton Club. It reopened again later in the year on Broadway at 48th Street, and the Hopkins band never played there.

With all of the prestige attached to the Cotton Club, the broadcasting schedule couldn't compare to the exposure a band got at Roseland. The network programs, although nationwide, were late-night broadcasts, and the saturation of the New York metropolitan audience by local radio stations in prime listening time, which helped make the band so popular at Roseland, was lost.

Probably the strangest wrinkle in the saga of the Claude Hopkins Orchestra is the question of why, after a prolific period of recording in 1933 and 1934, it made hardly any records in 1935, none at all in 1936, and only a handful in 1937. Aside from the three titles recorded for Decca in February of 1935, the band made no sides for the domestic market in that year, and the material since collected and released on LPs came from radio transcription dates. In other words, none of their music was available to the average record buyer.

It's difficult to understand this situation. The band was at the peak of its popularity, working at the most prestigious location in Harlem and broadcasting regularly on the CBS radio network. Furthermore, records and the recording industry were on the threshold of a fantastic resurgence, and records quickly assumed a vital role in building and maintaining a band's popularity. This was brought about by two important developments: the marketing of inexpensive electric turntables and tonearms, which could be connected to a radio, thus making it possible for the listener to enjoy the full range of the music, to the same extent that he could with radio broadcasts and at an affordable price; and the emergence of a new kind of radio personality called a "disc jockey."

The record players were just the beginning of the technical revolution that is still going on in the industry, but disc jockeys of the distinction of Martin Block, in New York, and Al Jarvis, in California, who conceived the idea of a Make Believe Ballroom, became major figures in the big-band business. In *WNEW, Where the Melody Lingers On: 1934–1984*, Nightingale Gordon wrote:

> The format of the program never changed. Employing the gentle fiction that each record was a live performance, Block welcomed popular bands and singers to an imaginary ballroom with a revolving stage. Each performer stayed under the crystal chandelier for 15 minutes. Millions of people visualized the ballroom in the theater of their imagination. . . .
> Block's Friday night preview of new releases, Saturday morning top-20 countdowns, and the semi-annual popularity polls carried enormous weight with listeners, artists and record companies. Programs like Make Believe Ballroom seemed to create hit records, and disc jockeys soon became the major promotion channel for the phonograph industry.

This was no exaggeration. In 1935, the year Martin Block began his broadcasts from the Crystal Ballroom, the bands entered into a new era, in which the phonograph record became as important as radio in building a band's popularity. A recording contract became an essential part of the business, and just about every name band of the period had one. All, it would seem, with the exception of Claude Hopkins. Why?

Along with the influence of the disc jockeys—and just about every radio station in every city and town had them, and still do—the coin-operated phonograph, better known as the juke box, came into its own, and hardly a bar, restaurant, diner, or ice-cream parlor was without one. The number of plays a hit record received in a given week became a subject of national interest, and it hardly seems necessary to point out what this meant to the band that recorded it. Or, for that matter, what a great mistake it was on the part of any band and its management to ignore this market.

At this stage it is practically impossible to fix responsibility for this tremendous oversight. Rockwell-O'Keefe was still handling the band and must share some of the blame. Cork O'Keefe would make no commitment on the subject, saying it was not in his jurisdiction with the company, and certainly Claude Hopkins can't be considered blameless because he had to be aware of what was going on. But placing the blame is no longer important. What does take on added dimension is the simple truth that this neglect at such a critical time may well have been the beginning of the end for the Hopkins band. There's no question that from 1935 on, records were a necessary part of the band business, and to be without a recording contract was downright foolish. Somebody completely missed the boat.

The

Beginning

of the

End

On the Road Again

Shortly before the band left the Cotton Club, Edmond Hall and Claude Hopkins had a falling out. Late in 1935, probably in December, Hall left Hopkins, with whom he had been for exactly six years. As quoted in *Profoundly Blue,* by Manfred Selchow, Fred Norman recalled: "Hall was a wonderful person. I've never seen him angry. The only time I saw him angry was when he left the Hopkins band. We were at the Cotton Club, you know. Ed had a little misunderstanding with Hopkins; he wanted to take him to the Union . . . money, or something like that."

Hall's place was taken by Chauncey Haughton, according to Norman, who also mentioned that Haughton played excellent clarinet as well as sax.

The Canadian tour in 1936 took the band to almost every principal city—Montreal, Ottawa, Peterborough, Toronto, Hamilton, Kitchener, London, Windsor—and finally wound up in Detroit. During the swing they sometimes spent two or three days at a location and in this way managed to squeeze in several college dates.

In Detroit they played a week at a downtown theater and then moved on to work at another national landmark in the music business, the famous Graystone Ballroom, once the home of the great Jean Goldkette band, with Bix Beiderbecke and Frank Trumbauer, and also McKinney's Cotton Pickers. The Hopkins crew attracted such huge crowds that people spilled into the annex from the main ballroom.

This triumph was followed by a quick trip to Chicago, where they played the Regal Theater and the Oriental Theater. The Chicago stay was highlighted for Claude by a big dinner party given in his honor by Earl Hines, which was attended by a number of local notables and attracted some nice write-ups in the newspapers.

Chicago became home base for the band for about a month while they filled engagements in the surrounding territory—Milwaukee, Evanston, Gary, and Fort Wayne—returning to Chicago after each date. When it came time to move on they hit Indianapolis, Dayton, Columbus, and Cincinnati, where they worked at a famous spot just across the Kentucky state line called the Lighthouse. Following this they commenced a southern swing that gradually brought them to the West Coast. A week in Sacramento was succeeded by another in Oakland, then a string of dancehalls and theaters in Los Angeles, and a brief stay at the Golden Gate Theater in San Francisco. They also played a number of dates outside the city and hated to leave the area because everywhere they went they were extremely well received.

The tour was extensive as well as profitable. All of the bookings had to be honored, so there were more one-nighters in Tacoma and Seattle, and even in the sparsely populated Dakotas. These jumps involved quite a bit of road travel and in the main were long, boring trips through miles of unrelieved prairie land, with scarcely anything worth looking at. One trip, however, was to leave a lasting impression.

They were booked to play a date in South Dakota, and the road they had to travel ran straight through mile after mile of a fenced-in range, which was all part of a huge government reservation for herds of bison. Signs posted at frequent intervals along the road warned travelers to stay in their cars because the bison bulls could be nasty and dangerous.

They were riding in a hired bus well past its prime, and in the middle of nowhere, with not a soul or a building in sight, it developed motor trouble and died. While the driver worked on the engine, the musicians decided to get out of the bus to stretch their legs and stood around talking and idly watching a herd of bison grazing in the near distance. The scene seemed very peaceful and bucolic—so much so that one musician was inspired to sing a few lines from "Home on the Range."

After a while Claude's attention was drawn to the movements of an unusually large bull. Over a period of several minutes it had quietly managed to drift closer and closer to where the band was standing and the bus was parked.

"Everybody back in the bus!" Claude told the men in a low but urgent tone, keeping a watchful eye on the big bull. "I think our friend over there is getting ready to make a personal call."

The huge bison was shaking his head in irritation and pawing at the ground. The musicians wasted no time in reboarding the bus, but that made no difference to the bull. It was the bright yellow bus that was the object of his attention. He obviously regarded it as an intruder in his domain and strongly resented its presence.

While the men on the bus stared out of the windows and watched in amazement—and not a little trepidation—the pugnacious animal lowered its head, seemed to gather its strength like an athlete about to perform a difficult feat, and charged the bus. He hit the vehicle broadside, rocking it from side to side to a chorus of yells and expletives from the passengers, and then loped away. But he wasn't finished. All he wanted was enough distance to build up another burst of speed, and after traveling several yards he turned and got ready for another charge. This time nobody on the bus took his intentions lightly. The animal probably weighed around 3,000 pounds and under a full head of steam was capable of wrecking the bus, even overturning it, and here they were miles from the nearest town or habitation.

All they could do was watch in anxious fascination as the big bull worked himself up for another charge. He stood shaking his head and snorting threats at the yellow interloper taking up space in his private domain, getting more aggravated every second because his threats didn't scare the bus away. But while he was making up his mind how to accomplish the most damage, the bus driver managed to get the engine started, jumped into the driver's seat, and put the bus in gear.

None too soon! The bull, furious at seeing his quarry about to escape, went into an all-out galloping charge, but all he could do was sideswipe the bus as it went by. The last the band saw of him he was still standing in the road shaking his head in fury and frustration, but he had earned their respect and made a very deep impression. The physical evidence was in the form of a huge dent in the side of the bus.

The Hopkins musicians shared another new experience that week in a little South Dakota town. They ate bear steaks, a local delicacy. Claude found them to be quite tasty.

As the western tour continued, the band played Omaha, Sioux Falls, Sioux City, and then put in a week at the Dance Palace in Denver. In St.

Louis they worked for Jessie Johnson, the big promoter in that area, and put in a ten-day stint at Hyland Park, one of the largest amusement parks in that part of the country. On the final leg, a swing designed to take them back to New York, they again hit St. Louis, playing the local "Cotton Club," then moved on to St. Joseph, Kansas City, Topeka, and all the principal cities of Ohio. They played theater dates in Pittsburgh and Philadelphia before making the final jaunt back to New York.

Fred Norman was still in the band when it made one of the western tours. In a personal interview, he said:

Claude was a wonderful guy. I remember one kind of funny incident. At the time when Jabbo [Smith] was the trumpet player in the band, the trombone section was Vic Dickenson, Floyd Brady, and myself. I think Sylvester Lewis was still in the band. Anyway, we went somewhere—like out to Ohio—and when we finished the gig that night and got on the bus, Claude told us, "Fellows, I'm going to talk all the way to Detroit"— or wherever it was we were going, I forget exactly where. He said, "I'm going to talk all the way there."

And, no kidding, he stood up in front of the bus and told stories, and talked and talked and when we finally got to our destination he could only whisper because he had lost his voice. Everybody cracked up, and told him, "You did it, man, but you lost your voice."

We had a lot of fun because we were a close-knit bunch of people. The thing I remember most about Claude was he might have had his faults, but he enjoyed life. He lived good, and he was one helluva musician. I have always felt that if he had stuck to his writing he would have done marvelously well, but he was essentially a player and a leader. I know, because he could whip that band into shape, and such things as tempos were always perfect.

In his notes Claude wrote: "The same routine prevailed—going into Roseland after a road tour—for '37, '38, '39, and part of '40." However, we enter a gray area here. The *Down Beat* and *Metronome* listings are consistent for the monthly "On Tour" feature until May 1939. That month's issue of *Down Beat* carries the cryptic notation, "(Apollo) NYC t, 5/5." Apparently Claude and his band were due to open at the Apollo Theater on the fifth. Following this the band isn't listed any more. At no point during the years following the Cotton Club engagement is Roseland listed. Fred Norman had no recollection of returning to Roseland but admitted the band may have played there for short periods when it was in New York. At the same time, he was under the impression that ownership of Roseland had changed, Lew Brecker was out, and Claude's connection with the place was finished. Fred's principal recollection of the rest of his term with the band was that it was constantly on the road.

There doesn't seem to be any question about the road tours. Claude's notes say, "I got rid of the bus and bought three new Dodges and a Dodge truck especially equipped to handle the instruments, uniforms, and other equipment including portable platforms and a small piano. By this time I had made several changes in the band and had added a very talented singer, who played a wonderful piano, Beverly White."

One night at the Savoy Ballroom in Chicago, for some reason Claude was late in getting to the bandstand. The band was already on stage waiting, so to be helpful Beverly sounded an A on the piano so the men could tune up. An over-zealous official from the International Office of the American Federation of Musicians saw her do it, and during the first intermission he was backstage checking union cards. When he discovered that Beverly White didn't have a card, he informed Claude he intended to bring the entire band up on charges, maintaining they had violated a strict union rule against permitting a nonunion musician to play with them. He also told Claude that he would see to it they paid the maximum fine for the offense, $300 for Claude and $100 for every man in the band.

Claude tried to explain that Beverly never played with the band and was only helping the men tune up, but the official refused to listen and put in the charges as he had promised. Claude's only recourse was to appeal the charges with the International Office, and although this didn't result in getting the charges dropped, it did succeed in reduced fines, so he wound up paying only $25 for himself and $5 for each of the others.

In the summer of 1937 Hopkins changed agencies and signed with the William Morris office, which booked the band until 1940, when Claude changed to Harold Oxley. Oxley also booked Jimmie Lunceford and was his manager. The bandleader makes no explanations for the changes, so we can only conjecture that he was dissatisfied with bookings and money. Possibly, the successful tour of 1936, made while the band was still riding its popularity from Cotton Club radio broadcasts, was followed by others that began to suffer from the lack of recordings and radio exposure. The public has a notoriously short memory. It doesn't take long for past glories to fade. While the Claude Hopkins Orchestra was on the road, other bands were broadcasting from choice locations and turning out records that were being reviewed in magazines and newspapers, thus keeping their names on display.

Metronome, a music magazine, and *Down Beat,* a tabloid publication in the 1930s, were the main sources of news and information about musicians and the musical organizations of the time, and they did a thorough job of reporting the goings-on in all facets of the business. Both publications reviewed record releases, theater and location appearances, and even radio broadcasts by the big bands. In addition, a good deal of space was devoted to news items pertaining to the goings and comings of musicians in and out of bands, various upheavals in the business, and general coverage of the entire music scene. Some of the biggest names—

Ellington, Goodman, Shaw, Herman, Basie—were constantly in print, but a good many others managed to get an occasional mention. Notably absent are references to the Claude Hopkins outfit, indicating that the same short-sighted policy that kept the band from making records was doing an equally bad job of publicity.

Although the overall economic climate was in favor of the bands, and business was good, it was also highly competitive and, as the country began to climb out of the Depression, increasingly costly. It wasn't unusual for some groups to maintain backup organizations larger than the bands they supported and serviced, and it took a lot of money to maintain them. In any case, these outfits were tough competition for the small fry—the leaders with less capital or no backers. Even though prominent sidemen began to organize and front their own bands with increasing frequency, this only succeeded in making the field more crowded, more competitive, and more expensive for many of the bands that had been around for years, offsetting whatever advantage there was to the increased demand for bands.

Claude Hopkins was understandably reticent about the last days of his band, and his notes gloss over the period quickly. We can only infer that a number of things may have contributed to the band's breakup in 1940—a fall-off in bookings, a sharp increase in expenses, and quite possibly, sheer weariness of life on the road. Then too, there were some indications that business wasn't as good in some places as was generally believed. For example, a short item in the July 1939 *Down Beat,* datelined Chicago, reported that the famous Grand Terrace Ballroom, long a resident location for the great Earl Hines band, had closed in June because of poor business, and the Hines band had taken to the road.

Whatever the reasons, as the decade was coming to an end Claude Hopkins's career was slowing down too. There was a brief spurt of life in October of 1938 when somebody arranged for the band to record a few sides for Vocalion under Ovie Alston's name, but nothing at all in 1939. The final swan song, the session for the short-lived Ammor label in February of 1940, demonstrates a band that had yielded to the contemporary trend toward slight, riff-oriented instrumentals with a series of ad-lib solos, coupled with an obvious bid for the commercial market with some pallid and undistinguished ballads. Not that this was out of the ordinary, since recording directors—later known as A & R men—as a rule had more to say about the material a band recorded than the bandleader, and every band was made to record things they wouldn't have if left to their own decisions.

Still, it can't be overlooked that when the band finally did record it was for a label with little or no distribution, and the sides were no help in keeping the band going. It fell apart in the latter part of the year, and the May 1, 1941, edition of *Down Beat* carried this brief item:

Once a Big Name, Hopkins Now Bankrupt

New York—Just a few years ago Claude Hopkins was one of the top men in the sepia band department. His orchestra, paced by his own nimble-fingered piano capers, was rated equally as good a box-office attraction as Ellington, Calloway and the rest.

Two weeks ago, in N.Y. Federal Court, Hopkins filed a voluntary petition in bankruptcy. He claimed his liabilities amounted to $3,770 and his assets $10,866. Hopkins said he owed his musicians $295 and the Wm. Morris agency $750. His assets include $2,741 in debts owed him, $4,000 in insurance policies, and $4,050 in exempt properties.

Hopkins hasn't been very active as a band leader in recent years, although in the middle '30's his records were best sellers and his band was a favorite at such spots as the Roseland on Broadway.

The War at Home

After all the years he had fronted a band, the very idea of being without one was difficult for Claude to accept. He felt naked and helpless—deprived of his livelihood and the career he had worked so hard and for so many years to develop. Then after some desperate soul-searching for a way out of the dilemma, calmer thinking took over and he decided the easiest and most logical move was to fall back on his ability as an arranger.

From time to time through the years, he had contributed arrangements to other bands and singers, so now—with considerable help and advice from Fred Norman, who left the band in 1938 to work full time as an arranger—it was fairly easy to line up some steady accounts.

Norman recalled: ∙

By that time I was doing work for CBS radio, and I had opened my office at 1650 Broadway, and Claude used to come down. So I told him, "Do some charts." I introduced him to the musical director at CBS—that is, the librarian—a Mr. Julius Matfell, who was a wonderful man, and he put Claude to work. But Claude scored in concert—as though he was writing parts for one great big piano, instead of the different keys suitable for each instrument—and that made the copying very expensive. But he contributed things for a number of programs on CBS.

In addition, as 1941 came around Claude was writing material for Tommy Tucker's band, Abe Lyman's, and some of the smaller groups like Louis Jordan's and John Kirby's, plus some vocal charts for the Boswell Sisters, Bea Wain, and the Murphy Sisters.

For the most part, aside from the tedious aspect of the work, arranging wasn't too difficult for him, but when he was handed an assignment to write for Phil Spitalny's renowned All Girl Orchestra, a twenty-seven-piece unit with a lot of strings, he had to ask for help. Once again it was the ever-faithful Fred Norman who came to the rescue with a few tricks of the trade and some shortcuts. Claude elaborated on this in *The World of Swing,* also crediting the symphony arrangers working at CBS with helpful suggestions.

By this time, however, he was already beginning to wear thin under the strain. It was one thing to write for his own band, at his own pace, and when he felt in the mood—and quite another to do it for a living. He found the routine to be too exacting and tiring. Even more important at the time, arranging for musical organizations, as honored and respected it might be as a peacetime occupation, had a low priority rating with draft boards. Claude was thirty-eight years old. In his own estimation he was a bit long in the tooth for service in the army, but he wasn't old enough to prevent his draft board from classifying him 1A for the next call-up, if they were so inclined, so he decided to look for an occupation more in tune with the times, such as a job in a defense plant.

With this in mind, he enrolled for a course in aircraft construction at a school in Yonkers, and after some four hundred hours of training, he graduated with an "above average" rating in all categories. With such qualifications, getting a job in a defense plant in 1942 was easy, and he was assigned to the Eastern Aircraft factory (formerly the General Motors assembly facility) in Linden, New Jersey.

Claude had always had a mechanical aptitude, and now it came in handy. He enjoyed the work he was doing, became pretty expert at it, and before long was moved up the ladder. He was made an inspector of the Tab controls on the Wildcat fighter plane used by the navy, a position of considerable responsibility. "Tab" was the trade name for the aerolon section of the tail and wing assembly, which controlled the ship in flight. A malfunction due to faulty construction could have tragic consequences.

Just about the time he had grown used to the idea of working at this job as long as the war continued, his normal routine was interrupted by a summons to appear at the front office. Since he wasn't told what it was about, he went up expecting the worst, even though he couldn't think of anything he had done that would get him into trouble. Instead of any work problems, it turned out that the big brass wanted his help.

As they explained it, every other airplane factory in the country had its own band or orchestra for the entertainment and recreation of the workers. Eastern didn't have any, and since Claude's reputation as a musician and bandleader was well known, the bosses wanted to know if he would be willing to put an organization together for them.

Claude agreed to try. He suggested they put notices on the bulletin boards throughout the plant and covering the three working shifts of the twenty-four-hour day, requesting that any musicians among the workers who were interested in playing in the plant's new band should tell the foreman of their shift their names and what instruments they played. The foreman would pass on the information to the front office, which in turn would give it to Claude for further action.

The suggestion was promptly put into play, and before long Claude was handed a list of over seventy-five names of people expressing interest in the project. The next step was to audition them, and the enthusiasm was such that the plant union volunteered the use of its meeting hall for the auditions. Claude wrote, "After I auditioned everybody on my own shift, I started coming into work an hour early so I could check out the other shifts, and finally through this long-drawn-out process of elimination I came up with 35 musicians with talent and experience."

If Claude had been left alone to complete the organizing in his own way, the plant would probably have had a band to be proud of. But as is so often the case when too many people are involved at the top, the well-intentioned idea backfired. Even before Claude had completed his auditions, somebody in the company decided it would be a great feather in their collective hat if they put together a transcription utilizing material from Claude's earlier career as a bandleader, and he was notified they intended to fly him to Detroit to work on the idea.

Whoever dreamed up the idea failed to take into consideration the bitter rivalry that existed between the defense plants, and somewhere along the line somebody raised strenuous objections. This resulted in certain GM officials' insisting that if any such project was to be done in Detroit, it had to be done by Detroit people, and, even more ridiculous, that somebody else be hired to emulate Claude on the transcription. When he first heard about it, Claude was steaming, but after a while the boondoggle struck him as funny, and he called his copy of the transcription "one of my most cherished possessions."

While things were developing with the plant orchestra, it became clear that the idea was more visionary and ambitious than practical. As soon as Claude began calling for rehearsals, he ran into trouble. In all the other defense plants it was customary for the company to allot an hour or so of company time for rehearsals, but the management at Eastern refused, and when the decision was passed down to the volunteer musicians the entire band quit.

So Claude went back to his job as Tab inspector, a bit annoyed that so much of his time and effort had been wasted, but secretly relieved that the project hadn't worked out. He was content to do his job and forget about it.

Then along came another problem—this time a major one—which developed out of a trifling incident. Harold G. Hoffman, who had been governor of New Jersey for several terms before the war and was commissioned a lieutenant colonel in the army, came through the Eastern facility on a tour of the plant. He was accompanied by his wife. When they got to Claude's section they stopped to have their picture taken with him, and the picture wound up on the cover of the monthly GM plant magazine—much to the dissatisfaction of a certain plant foreman.

After the magazine appeared, the foreman began to needle Claude every time they met, making snide remarks about the "big shot" and other comments designed to get under his skin. This went on for some time until Claude, never too long on patience, had all he could take. They had a fight, and since the foreman had the rank and some seniority, Claude was the one who got fired. Automatically this meant he was back to being classified 1A for the draft—and the war was at its height.

"I still didn't like the idea of going into the army at my age," he wrote, "so after thinking things over I decided to try the navy."

Some inquiries regarding the right people to contact brought him an address in Washington, and he sat down to compose a long letter reviewing his background and experience, and requesting an assignment commensurate with his abilities. After some anxious waiting he got a reply in the form of a request for publicity pictures to be published in a navy paper, instructions on where to go for a physical examination, and the heart-warming information that he would be made a chief petty officer in charge of a band stationed in Cuba.

Naturally, Claude was elated. It all seemed so easy that he couldn't help berating himself for not taking the step sooner. It seemed the ideal solution to all his problems. And when he went for his physical he met another bandleader who had received the same instructions, Eddy Duchin. They went through the examination together, getting checked out by no less than twenty-two doctors before being certified as fit for duty.

The next step was a round of interviews with navy officers in New York and even a trip to Washington designated as official business by the navy department. Claude was told it was merely a case of waiting for the final decision and his appointment to come through. All indications were positive, they assured him, but the wait was agonizing, and Claude felt like a kid waiting for Christmas morning.

After quite a bit of time had elapsed without a hint or a word, the mailman delivered an official-looking envelope from the Navy Department. No kid ever ripped open a Christmas present faster than Claude tore into that envelope. Based upon what he had been told, he fully expected a confirmation of his appointment and instructions on when and where to report for duty, but as he read the letter his elation turned to bitter disappointment.

Apologetically, the writer explained that due to recent adverse publicity and resulting scandal concerning the appointment of navy commissions, the secretary of war had immediately put a stop to all appointments. The letter went on to suggest that if Claude enlisted in the navy through regular channels it was fairly certain he would quickly be promoted and appointed to the kind of assignment he had applied for.

Somehow Claude couldn't bring himself to put much confidence in the suggestion, especially after the way things had fallen apart following all the promises and assurances. He decided to forego any further dealings with the navy, even though it meant he was back to square one with his draft board. Now that negotiations with the navy were over, the board would be breathing down his neck.

The idea of being drafted into the army, even at this late date, wasn't pleasant, but he had a more immediate concern—a job. He didn't have one, and no money was coming in. From every angle, the outlook was gloomy.

The Club Zanzibar and USO Tours

In 1944, after his misadventure with the navy, Claude landed a job at the Club Zanzibar, an opportunity that couldn't have come along at a more fortuitous time. The journal notes: "A syndicate that owned several nightclubs in New York was opening a new club, the 'Club Zanzibar,' at 49th and Broadway. Joe Howard, the manager, called me and wanted to know how long it would take to get a 15-piece band in shape. I told him about two weeks, at the least. At the time I didn't know where I could get the men for a band, because the war had grabbed so many musicians, but surprisingly, in a couple of days I had more men than I could use."

If the personnel the journal lists is correct, the band turned out to be an eleven-man unit with a female vocalist. It included Kenneth Roane and Courtney Williams, trumpets; Floyd Brady, trombone; Rudy Powell, Joe Garland, Skippy Williams, and Pinky Williams, reeds; John Brown, bass; Wilbur Kirk, drums; Eddie Gibbs, guitar; Claude on piano; and a vocalist, Marie Ellington.

Claude wrote: "This outfit was one of my best bands, I think, for sound quality and ability."

They went into rehearsals for the floor show at the club, but Claude was worried about other commitments: "The real problem was getting a library together, because we were scheduled to do a lot of broadcasting, and also play for dancing. Joe Howard immediately engaged about five top arrangers, and before the opening we had ten or fifteen beautiful arrangements. The men in the band were very cooperative, because besides rehearsing so very hard for the show, we had to rehearse the dance numbers."

The show, which ran for the next six to eight months, included many of the biggest names in show business and got off to a good start. On the bill were the Ink Spots, Ella Fitzgerald, Stump and Stumpie (a head-line comedy and dance team), the great Bill "Bojangles" Robinson, the Berry Brothers, Howell and Bowser, and sixteen chorus girls plus eight beautiful picture girls.

In the beginning Claude played piano with the band, but as the show began to demand more and more of his time for directing he brought in Eddie Bonimere to fill the piano spot. Meanwhile, the band's library kept growing. Claude hired some more outside arrangers to make contributions and paid his trumpet player, Courtney Williams, a bonus for turning in one chart a week. Once in a while he wrote one himself. With this constant building, they eventually wound up with forty or fifty numbers in the book. It was an exciting time, and Claude plunged into his work wholeheartedly, no longer worrying about the draft board, deciding to let matters take their own course without further efforts to force his luck.

Of his years at the Club Zanzibar, Claude wrote: "Sometimes when the show changed and new attractions were brought in, I'd try revamping the band's instrumentation—such as using five saxes, one trumpet, and three rhythm. This kept things interesting. Anyway, I kept busy, even writing arrangements for the show from time-to-time, and we played the Zanzibar from 1944 to 1947, when it finally closed. Another club opened at the same location later, under a different name."

By 1947 there was no longer any danger of Claude's being drafted, but the war years and other social and economic upheavals had done irrevocable damage to the big-band business. Although musicians returning from the services were under the illusion they could take up where they left off and things would return to prewar status, they were due for a rude awakening.

Changes that had actually begun before the war, such as the ascendancy of vocalists over the bands in popularity and on records, continued to develop. This trend was largely a result of the recording strike put into effect by James C. Petrillo, president of the musicians' union, in the early 1940s and the union's feud with the radio networks, which resulted in the curtailment of a great number of the remote location broadcasts, once the lifeblood of the dance-band business. Costs continued to escalate, and a previously unheard-of factional division grew between advocates of a new music form variously known as "rebop," "bebop," and finally just "bop" and those who remained loyal to the traditional styles. These and other trends chipped away at the fragile structure that supported the big bands. It wasn't long before it became painfully obvious to all those who were interested that whatever remained of the music business was for small groups.

Claude was quick to recognize the trend, and after the Club Zanzibar closed he organized a quartet, with Scoville Brown on clarinet and tenor; Eddie Gibbs, guitar; and John Brown, bass. With himself on piano and a vocalist named Rena Collins, they made some records for a new company called Rainbow Records. To everybody's surprise the records clicked well enough to spur interest in the group, bookings opened up, and once again Claude was on the road.

This time Claude bought a big Chrysler for the group to tour in, and they played clubs in Cleveland, Chicago, Washington, Baltimore, and New York. Then Van Alexander—a fine arranger and bandleader in his own right—began booking attractions for the Sheraton hotel chain. He set up the Hopkins group with a job in a hotel in Worcester, Massachusetts, on a contract that called for an eight-week stay with an option. The group did so well the option was picked up, and they worked there for four months. This was followed by dates in every one of the Sheraton hotels with a music policy. The circuit took them to Providence, Boston, and Springfield. The work was easy and enjoyable, and it lasted until 1949.

At this point Claude became involved in something he came to regard as one of the most rewarding experiences of his long career. It began with a phone call from the USO—the organization established to provide entertainment for the men and women of the armed forces and in service hospitals all over the country as well as overseas—and an offer to lead a unit in a nine-month tour of every veteran's hospital in the United States. The idea appealed to Claude, and he accepted the offer. He recalled:

We played in the hospital auditoriums, usually in the afternoon but sometimes in the evening, depending on the hospital's schedule, and then afterwards we always went through the wards where the wounded were confined to their beds, moving the piano along on big, rubber-tired wheels from one ward to another. The shows we put on weren't very big. Generally they consisted of a four- or five-piece band, a danceteam, a comedy team, a singer, and maybe a chorus line of five or six girls who could also sing. This last is what the men would enjoy the most, along with the comedy, and it was heart-warming the way they would cheer us afterwards, acting as if nothing was wrong with them. It made you feel very small complaining about things that were nothing compared to their problems and afflictions.

Altogether it was one of the most interesting tours I have ever taken, and we were afforded a first-hand look-see at the positively phenomenal work the doctors were doing. You really had to see it to believe it. It was also gratifying to see that the hospitals were equipped with facilities to provide all kinds of entertainment for the patients, from first-run movies to recreation rooms with everything from tiddly winks to bowling alleys.

Claude found this tour so rewarding that he repeated it in 1950, happy to find that many of the patients he remembered meeting the first time around had gone home to lead normal lives. He also found it somewhat gratifying that even those who were destined to remain in the hospitals for the rest of their lives were provided with every comfort and convenience, almost to the extent of living in a luxury resort.

Speaking of his father's USO performances, Claude Hopkins, Jr., said: "He got quite a few commendations for it. He really contributed quite a bit to his country during the war, and he contributed quite a bit before and after the war."

Chorus Girls

With so many years of road tours under his belt, living out of suitcases and putting up with a myriad of inconveniences, Claude—now nearing the mid-century mark—might have been more than ready to forego life on the road and stay close to home. Instead he teamed up with his old friend E. C. Hill, and they formed a partnership to build a road show suitable for theaters in the South.

To take care of bookings they retained an office headquartered in Charlotte and managed by T. D. Kemp, a brother of the late Hal Kemp, who led a famous orchestra in the 1930s. Kenneth Harris became their producer and contact man.

As usual, in the beginning it all looked easy. The partners had no trouble lining up acts, both comedy and novelty. But when they got to the part of building the show that was expected to be the easiest, hiring girls for the chorus line, they ran into trouble. When Harris contacted girls with experience they asked for more money than the budget could afford. Claude had been given a top figure and couldn't go over it.

The partners were nonplussed. Chorus girls had never been a problem before. In the old days there were always more applicants than there were available jobs, but like so many other things after the war, the situation had changed drastically. As ridiculous as it seemed to Claude, the chorus girl problem threatened to scuttle the production before it could get started. He was ready to give up in disgust, when Ken Harris came up with an inspiration.

Why worry about paying big salaries to get girls with experience? He would go into the garment district, where he was certain there were hundreds of girls with talent who would jump at the chance to get into show business. All he had to do was dangle the offer.

As it turned out, he was absolutely right, and in a couple of days he had recruited eight candidates for the chorus line. They were pretty girls and willing, and some were even talented, but only two of them had the slightest idea of how to dance. This created another crisis and brought on a series of long and hard rehearsals. Because the same stingy budget prohibited the rental of a rehearsal hall, Claude volunteered the use of the recreation room in his home, which was fitted out with a piano and a sound system.

Claude thought the show routine wasn't very complicated. Consisting of an opening number, a middle, and a finale, it should have come together quickly. Instead, as the deadline for taking the production on the road crept uncomfortably close, the inexperienced showgirls were making it difficult to whip the show into shape.

After a while it was decided to let four of the girls go as completely hopeless, leaving the other four as a rather skimpy chorus line. Claude considered six girls the minimum necessary for a decent-looking chorus line. He was to the point of asking Harris to make another foray into the garment district when one of the feature acts in the show, a trio of girls— Dabs, Cherry, and Candy—volunteered to supplement the chorus line in addition to doing their own act. This was a big break. Besides being beautiful, the girls were sensational dancers.

Even then, the production still wasn't out of the woods. The inexperienced girls kept forgetting the dance routines. Harris rehearsed them from seven o'clock in the evening until four or five in the morning, with coffee breaks of sandwiches and deviled eggs provided by Claude's wife, Mabel, but although the girls worked hard and conscientiously they didn't show much improvement.

Finally Harris and Hopkins had a conference and decided the show was as ready as it would ever be. They notified the cast to get ready to take to the road, Ed Hill bought two Pontiac station wagons with luggage racks on the roofs, and they were all set. Claude wrote, "For better or worse we were off to the southland—rented costumes and all!"

They opened to a good crowd and were well received, even though the inexperienced girls got such bad stage fright they forgot everything they had been taught. But as the show moved from town to town they got over it and settled down to doing a fair job.

For the most part the show played one-night engagements and never stayed more than three nights in one place. Then, before they realized what was happening, they were pioneering something new. T. D. Kemp began booking them into first-class white houses where black entertainers had never appeared before, and he was getting such favorable comments that other promoters and theater managers were asking for bookings. These dates were very profitable, but unfortunately there weren't enough theaters of this kind to keep the show busy. They were forced to supplement them with stops in the black houses, most of which had never been intended to handle anything other than movies. They were so small that even playing three shows a day to capacity audiences wasn't enough to cover expenses. As a result the show was constantly skirting the edge of a financial hole.

Some weeks the receipts were pretty good, and they were able to pay their way. But then they ran into a spell of bad weather—a near disaster in the rural South because it presented serious transportation problems. The receipts fell off so badly it put the partnership in the red, and they were never able to make up the deficit, even though the entire cast agreed to take a cut in salary. The lack of money made people despondent, a natural reaction, and the partners were hard put to keep up morale.

Nevertheless, somehow the show managed to hold together for another four or five months, constantly in trouble, but desperately trying to hang on long enough to take advantage of the good period of the year, from September to February. Finally they reached Winston-Salem, and at that point the partners agreed that since they weren't getting anywhere, it was time to call it quits.

They sent everybody home, sold the station wagons, and did what they could to forget their own financial losses. Oddly enough, it wasn't the loss of money that was Claude's biggest regret, it was having to scrap the show, a production that by then had developed, in his words, into "a pretty fair unit."

Later, the partners decided their basic mistake was in not asking for and insisting on a bigger guarantee. Instead, they had agreed to a percentage deal, which in the smaller houses amounted to almost nothing, and this was their downfall. In the beginning they didn't realize what was happening and had to find out the hard way, but by the time they reached Winston-Salem, they knew they were licked.

Claude was only too happy to leave it all behind and head back to New York, but the tour had taken its toll. He was exhausted, both physically and mentally, and had to take a few months off to rest up.

Claude as a young man. Photo
courtesy of Flora Walden Chase.

Mabel Hopkins, circa 1924. Photo
from Hopkins collection.

La Revue Nègre, Paris, 1925. Left to right: Percy Johnson, Louis Douglas, Josephine Baker, Bass Hill, Hopkins, Joe Hayman, Daniel Doy. Photo courtesy of Frank Driggs Collection.

The Hopkins orchestra at Joe Ward's Swannee Club on 125th Street in New York, 1929–30. Left to right: Nelson Hurd, Sylvester Lewis, Pete Jacobs, Maceo Edward, Jo Jones, Hopkins, Henry Turner, Gene Johnson, Bobby Sands, Edmond Hall. Photo courtesy of Frank Driggs Collection.

Claude Hopkins and His Orchestra as they appeared in the 1933 movie short, *Barber Shop Blues*. Left to right: Walter Jones, Hopkins, Ovie Alston, Sylvester Lewis, Orlando Robeson, Albert Snaer, Pete Jacobs, Gene Johnson, Fred Norman, Henry Turner, Bobby Sands, Fernando Arbello, Edmond Hall. Photo courtesy of Frank Driggs Collection.

The Claude Hopkins band in *By Request*, a 1935 movie short. A number of changes have been made in the personnel. Left to right: Fred Norman, Edmond Hall (front), Henry Wells (behind), Bobby Sands, Hopkins, Walter Jones, Pete Jacobs, Ovie Alston, Gene Johnson, Sylvester Lewis, Hilton Jefferson, Russell Smith, Henry Turner. Photo courtesy of Frank Driggs Collection.

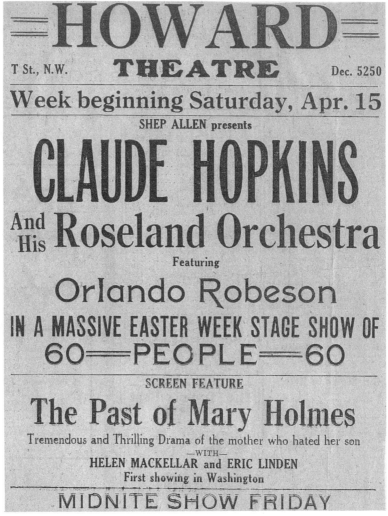

Howard Theatre advertisement. From Hopkins collection.

The popular Orlando Robeson at the mike in front of the Hopkins band at Roseland Ballroom, 1933. Eddie Williams, at far right, is subbing for Ed Hall. Photo courtesy of Frank Driggs Collection.

Roseland Ballroom, 1933, Hopkins at the piano. Left to right, front row: Ovie Alston, Orlando Robeson (sitting in for Sylvester Lewis), Albert Snaer, Walter Jones, Gene Johnson, Bobby Sands, Eddie Williams; left to right, rear: Fred Norman, Fernando Arbello, Pete Jacobs, Henry Turner. Photo courtesy of Frank Driggs Collection.

Claude Hopkins and His Orchestra, c. 1934. Left to right, back row: Abe Baker, Gene Johnson, Shirley Clay, Bobby Sands, Chauncey Douglas, Fred Norman, Lincoln Mills, Pete Jacobs; left to right, front row: Hopkins, Jabbo Smith, Vic Dickenson, Beverly White, Ben Smith, Walter Jones. Photo courtesy of Fred Norman.

Fred Norman. Photo courtesy of Fred Norman.

The Claude Hopkins Quartet with Rene Collins. This group recorded for Rainbow Records. Photo from the Hopkins collection.

In the recording studio with Juanita Hall to make a blues and jazz LP, 1957. Left to right: Doc Cheatham, Buster Bailey, Coleman Hawkins, Juanita Hall, Hopkins, George Duvivier, Jimmy Crawford. Photo courtesy of Frank Driggs Collection.

The Jazz Giants. Left to right, rear: Benny Morton, Herb Hall, Hopkins, Buzzy Drootin, Arvell Shaw. Wild Bill Davison is seated in front. Photo from Hopkins collection.

Mabel Hopkins with Claude Jr. at his confirmation, 1963.
Photo from Hopkins collection.

Claude Hopkins and Flora Walden Chase, 1973. Photo courtesy of
Flora Walden Chase.

Claude and granddaughter Sherene, 1973. Photo from Hopkins collection.

Study by an unknown photographer.
Photo from Hopkins collection.

Claude in about 1974. Photo by
Kathy Gardner.

The Beginning of the End

The Cotton Club was a favorite haunt of movie stars. Whenever John Barrymore was in New York he was good for two or three nights every week of his stay. Wallace Beery was another frequent visitor. This pleased Claude immensely because the rugged actor was his favorite movie star, and he had seen every picture Beery ever made.

The bandleader vividly recalled the first night Wallace Beery came into the club. Claude and the band were on the stand, but he spotted the actor immediately and looked around for something to write on so he could get the great man's autograph. Nothing was handy, so in desperation he took out his union card and asked Kid Griffin, the headwaiter, to take it to the actor's table and request his autograph.

Griffin performed the errand, but when he came back with the signed card he also brought word that Mr. Beery had requested that the band-leader visit at his table at the end of the set, because he wanted Claude to return the favor and give him his autograph. He later told Claude that he listened to every broadcast the band made and was a big fan.

Claude was thrilled: "Boy! did I feel honored! After that first meeting we got to be pretty good friends, and we had many chats about his

Mahogany Hall and the Nevele

When idleness ceased to be restful and just became monotonous, Claude organized another entertaining quartet—bass, guitar, and female singer—and went back to playing lounges in the Sheraton hotels. He did this for better than a year, then accepted an offer to join a little band that was playing jazz in a place called Mahogany Hall in Boston.

Mahogany Hall was one of two rooms in the Copley-Plaza Hotel operated as jazz clubs by George Wein. Storyville was upstairs, and Mahogany Hall, devoted to dixieland jazz, was in the basement. Storyville featured personalities such as Sarah Vaughan. The Mahogany Hall group included trumpeter Doc Cheatham, trombonist Vic Dickenson, the Drootin brothers, Buzzy and Al, and bassist Jimmy Woode. Claude stayed on for three years, from 1951 to 1953.

Doc Cheatham's wife gave birth to their son during this time, marking it in Doc's memory as special. He recalled the band as a very good one, and Claude Hopkins as "a very fine piano player, something in the mold of James P. Johnson. He had a terrific left hand."

When the job at Mahogany Hall folded, Claude returned to New York, where he gravitated to the great jazz being played by Henry "Red" Allen and his groups at the Metropole Cafe for a stint that lasted until 1960.

In my book, *This Horn for Hire,* Pee Wee Erwin gives a vivid description of this spot:

We were booked into one of the great phenomena of the music world of its time, the Metropole, located on Broadway between 48th and 49th in New York City. The original location had been a block south on Broadway, and at that time the place had a big-band policy. After the move was made to the new spot, it switched to the New Orleans format of the band playing on a stage behind the bar. The bar at the Metropole was one of the longest I've ever seen, so the band looked out over a sea of faces—not only those of the people seated at the bar but more who were seated at tables on the far side of the room. We were there during June and July so the glass doors facing Broadway were left wide open, and the music could be heard up and down the street for quite a distance, acting as a natural ballyhoo. . . . Actually we were filling in for the man who, in my opinion, more than anybody else was responsible for the Metropole's huge success, Henry "Red" Allen, fabulous trumpet player and entertainer.

Erwin was to work at the Metropole again. As quoted in *This Horn for Hire,* he said:

It seemed that business at the Metropole had expanded to the point where they were now presenting jazz from one in the afternoon until four in the morning, seven days a week. The main night attractions played from 9 PM until 4 AM. One group, under the leadership of Henry "Red" Allen, included J. C. Higginbotham, Claude Hopkins, Buster Bailey, and various drummers like Cozy Cole, Sticks Evans, and others of note.

This group impressed a lot of people—in particular, a young man who was to retain his memories of the Metropole for the rest of his life, Claude Hopkins, Jr.:

I can remember, when I was only five or six years old, visiting my father when he was working at the Metropole Cafe, and sitting on the bandstand watching him play and the other musicians perform. I used to really get a kick out of being around him. At the Metropole I was fascinated by the drummer, Cozy Cole, and I told my father that I wanted to be a drummer. But he always discouraged me about getting into music because of the kind of life he had to lead during his early days. He said it was an ordeal he didn't want me to have to endure. But even though he discouraged me, he let me take drum lessons, and I got pretty good at it, and he let me sit in with him on the stand at concerts and in the clubs.

At the time I first played I must have been about ten, and I got a big kick out of it. My fantasy was to one day have a band with my father and to play professionally. That never came about.

Claude Jr. was to become an important factor in the life of Claude Sr. from that time on, especially when the father moved on to another location job that was to last six years. He took a trio into a Catskill resort hotel in Ellenville, New York, called the Nevele and settled in for a long stay.

"I remember the first year he played at the Nevele," Claude Jr. recalled:

He came home during the holidays, and he was very happy. The owner of the hotel had taken a liking to my father and was very generous to him. My father told us how the owner had called him into his office (I think he had been at the hotel for a couple of months) and gave him five $100 bills for a Christmas present. Then the owner said, "You know, I enjoy your music throughout the year, so I want to share a little Christmas spirit with you." Then he went on to say, "You have a home here as long as you want it."

The trio at the Nevele included Shorty Baker on trumpet and Marquis Foster on drums, with vocalist Dolores Brown. "In my estimation Claude Hopkins was one of the giants of the piano," said Marquis Foster of the years at the Nevele. "His left hand was super. I learned a lot from Claude, especially about playing drums without a bass player. And with Shorty Baker and Dolores Brown we had a ball. Claude was a very dapper dresser, and very careful about his appearance; used cold cream to keep his hands soft. I can still hear him playing his theme song, "I Would Do Anything for You." But as quoted in *The World of Swing*, Claude himself passes over the period with only a brief and rather negative comment: "I went to the Nevele Country Club up in the Catskills. I stayed up in the mountains till '66, till I got tired of the woods and began to smell like an ear of corn."

Claude Jr.'s recollections were more pleasant and specific:

Back in the early sixties my father went to work at a country club in the Catskill Mountains called the Nevele, and I used to go up there every summer during recess, and on weekends and holidays. I liked to be around my father, and while all the other kids would be out playing or doing whatever kids will do at that age, I was happy to sit in the club and listen to my father. And sometimes he would let me sit in on the bandstand and play a couple of numbers.

My dad was the type of person who would take the shirt off his back to give to a total stranger. I mean, he would go out of his way to help somebody. He was an introverted person, and it was hard for him to express his feelings, but he showed them in other ways. Once he was supposed to come back to the city to pick me up and take me to the hotel for the weekend. I waited and waited, and I remember being very upset with him because he didn't show up. But when I found out why, although I was still disappointed at not being able to spend the weekend with him, I was proud of what he had done.

While traveling through the town of Ellenville on his way from the hotel, he saw an old wooden house on fire. There were a couple of elderly women living in the house, and they were trapped in the building. He went in to rescue the ladies, and while he was doing so part of the floor caved in and he injured his leg. So he was laid up for a short period of time, but this didn't stop him from performing, although it limited his driving for a while. He was awarded some kind of citation from the town of Ellenville, he was written up in the newspaper, and I was very proud of him.

I used to have a ball meeting all the entertainers and the up-and-coming stars that came to the club. I recall an aspiring young comedian who used to perform in the lounge where my father had his trio. I believe he was about twenty years old, and he was brought in by another comedian named Dave Asterwoods. Nobody knows what really happened to him, but Dave Aster (as he called himself) was supposed to become a big star, and Richard Pryor wasn't supposed to amount to anything.

Quite a few stars came through the doors of the Nevele, the Concord, Grossinger's—all the circuits in the area in those days—Norm Crosby, Totie Fields, Nipsy Russell, and many more I can't recall right now. There was a group called Hines, Hines, and Dad and Brown. This was the Hines brothers, their dad, and Johnny Brown. They used to come to the club and perform their show, but then the group broke up and they went their separate ways. Gregory Hines is a big star, and his brother is on Broadway.

I really was exposed to all aspects of show business at a very early age—the good and the bad.

My father loved animals, and he was fascinated by dogs. While he was working at the Nevele he was always worried about my mother and me being back in the city by ourselves. So he went out and bought me a Doberman pinscher, a beautiful animal trained by a professional trainer that would perform to commands. I mean, this animal was a thoroughbred! But when we brought him back to the city, my mother didn't want him. She had become paranoid about Dobermans because of a big news article in the paper about a New Jersey woman who was attacked and killed by her own dog. The dog was a Doberman and it devoured the woman. But as the article explained, the woman had taken the dog from her husband, who was a trainer and had trained the dog to be an attack dog, and tried to make a house pet out of it. I guess it couldn't stand being a pet to be kicked around and pushed, so it turned on the lady. And that's all my mother would talk about.

We brought the dog back to the city, and I kept it for a couple of months, but my mother was so afraid of it that she wouldn't even go into the kitchen by herself, where the dog was kept.

So we had to get rid of the dog. This was very upsetting to me, and my father was pretty disappointed. But usually whatever the wishes of my mother were, my father would respect them.

My mother and father had a very unique relationship. My mother knew the type of life that my father led, being in the band business. My father was far from being an angel or a saint, but he would always—even throughout all the lady friends he would encounter—he would always make sure home was taken care of first. As a kid growing up, I never remember going without anything. Maybe I had too much. My mother was a woman with very few needs. I mean, she just wanted the basics, and my father would want to shower her with all kinds of gifts. But she never wanted anything fancy—just the basic needs for everyday life.

I know she was aware of what my father was doing while he was on the road and away from her. But she sort of—I don't know—you might say she looked the other way, or tolerated it. He respected her, yet when he was on the road and working he had women at his feet. I mean, he would have ladies all over the place. But when he came back home it was like being in a different world.

Getting back to the time we were at the Nevele, I recall that things were going pretty good, and then—I believe it was during the mid-sixties—the Beatles invaded the United States. Well, that's when everybody went rock-and-roll crazy. That was the new fad. The manager of the club at the hotel suggested to my father that he change his style of playing to accommodate the rock-and-roll fans, and he refused. Then one thing led to another, and my father decided it was time to leave.

After he left they brought in a couple of rock groups, but this didn't go over too well with the older crowd, so then they opened up the room just for teenagers, and for a while the rock went over pretty good with them. But then most of the teenagers preferred the jukebox for dancing, so the rock died down, and at this point they asked my father to come back. And again he refused. I guess his pride was pretty strong, and he didn't feel he should go back.

Mahogany

Hall

and the

Nevele

The Jazz Giants and Solo Performances

After the six-year stint at the Nevele, Claude went back to New York and joined a group of star jazzmen to form a band with the flamboyant name of the Jazz Giants. Not that they didn't merit the title; they did. Every man in the group could point to a long and illustrious background in jazz stretching back to the early 1920s, and each one was a well-known name. The Jazz Giants included Wild Bill Davison, cornet; Benny Morton, trombone; Herb Hall, clarinet; Buzzy Drootin, drums; Arvell Shaw, bass; and Claude Hopkins, piano.

The band was successful right from the start, and for the next three years they made several trips a year to Toronto, Canada, and worked other locations in Boston, Cleveland, and Pittsburgh. They also recorded two albums for John Norris in Toronto (see the discography).

Claude Hopkins, Jr., recalled this period vividly:

During this time I traveled with my father for a summer. We went to Cleveland, Ohio, and they played at a club—I believe it was called the Theatrical Grill—on a strip there in Cleveland. It was a pretty exclusive place. A lot of ball players in town would come to the club, and I remember meeting Joe Louis there. Joe Louis and my father were close buddies, going back to when my father's band was pretty prominent and Joe Louis was in his prime. That was a thrill for me.

And the stories I heard about Joe Louis! He was a ladies' man. When he was leaving the club he had a blonde on one arm and a brunette on the other. I had to kind of rush to get his autograph.

I met quite a few people at the club—Emmett Ashford, the first black umpire, and Joe Pepitone. At that time the New York Yankees were playing in Cleveland, so I met a few of the ball players. They gave us tickets to the game, so we went to the stadium to watch the Yankees play Cleveland. I don't remember who won, though.

This was in the late sixties, during the summer when they had the big riot in Cleveland. It was during the period when the country was going through a lot of radical changes. They put a curfew on the town, and they were stopping every black person walking the streets. We were staying in the hotel, and on several occasions my father and I were stopped on the street and questioned by national guardsmen about our reason for being on the street. We were advised to stay inside the hotel and to stay away from windows. There were guards on every corner—armed guards. I mean, there was really a bad situation.

It was the first time for me to be caught right in the middle of a riot. I had been in towns where there were riots—on the outside looking in— but this was the first time being caught up in the middle of one. It was a very scary feeling. They closed the club down for a couple of days, clamped on the curfew, and we had to stay inside. Then they lifted the curfew, and my father went back to work.

It seemed to me that in every town we would go to, my father would have a female companion, either one he had just met, or one he knew from a previous time of passing through the town. They would be waiting for him when he came back.

From Cleveland we went to—I believe it was Boston—and a place called Lenny's on the Turnpike. It was a small club, but it was a pretty popular jazz spot. And I think it was around this time that my father and Wild Bill Davison started to have a few little problems about running the band. It was a conflict over who was really the leader. I remember my father saying he had all the responsibility of booking the engagements and all the responsibilities entailed in holding the group together, while Wild Bill wanted his name out front as the leader.

My father didn't care too much about that. You know, it didn't bother him because he had always had his own band and his name had always been up in big letters, sot hat really didn't bother him. But when the conflict started to interrupt the everyday flow of good music, that's when it started to be a problem

And there were others. Arvell Shaw is a great musician, but he is a very temperamental one. I remember him walking off the stand on several occasions right in the middle of a song, and my father would have to pamper him and baby him and kinda tell him things he wanted to hear, and then he would get back on the stand. But then they would get to the next show and it would start up again and they would have to go through their bit.

Running a band of any size never fails to create problems, both economical and personal, but Claude had a high opinion of Wild Bill and understood him much better than most people. In *The World of Swing,* Claude stated:

In recent years I've worked a lot with Wild Bill Davison. There isn't a nicer guy anywhere. He talks tough, but underneath he's got a big heart. He cried more than I did when I lost my wife. Of course, I had tears, but I've never been emotional. He isn't as strong as he used to be, but he's got a gift of the gab, and he talks with the customers, and they love it. When someone requests something he doesn't want to play, he says, "Get your own band."

Nevertheless, after the Jazz Giants broke up, Claude decided he'd had enough of running a band, as noted in the journal:

This experience made me decide to go it alone, which I prefer doing anyway. I played the Newport Jazz Festival for several seasons, did a number of concerts in New York and New Jersey and Connecticut, and several for the Smithsonian Institution in Washington. Then Tommy Gwaltney, former owner of "Blues Alley," put a trio together to open a new Ramada Inn in Alexandria, Virginia, my home town, so I joined him and stayed for quite awhile. Then I got a call from George Wein to make a tour of the various European jazz festivals—Nice, France; Germany; Switzerland; Spain; and Milan, Italy. This turned out to be a yearly thing, and is still going. In fact, every week there are more festivals.

Claude Jr. is more specific about his father's activities after the Jazz Giants called it quits:

My father went back to playing concerts and making guest appearances. He made a couple of albums and performed at several New York clubs.

For some time he played at Jimmy Ryan's, also Eddie Condon's, and at a place in Paterson, New Jersey, called the Three Sisters, plus a lot of other local clubs throughout the tri-state area. He was pretty content with this because it didn't take too much out of him and he was near home. He enjoyed playing, but the responsibilities entailed in running a big band and being on the road took a lot of the enjoyment away from him. This is why he was pretty content with making solo appearances.

My father didn't start to do any more extensive traveling until after my mother died. She died in January of 1972, the same year that I got married. My father was working at Jimmy Ryan's on the night she died, and I was home. I'll never forget it.

My mother's name was Mabel Hopkins, and she was a dancer. She used to travel with my father and his band, and she performed in the chorus. One of the stories he always told about her was that when they went to Europe back in the early 1920s—when he made that trip to Europe with the *Revue Nègre*, with Josephine Baker—the only way my mother could go along was to become a member of the revue. At the time my mother didn't know her left foot from her right, but a couple of members of the chorus took her to the side and gave her a few little instructions, and she got the steps down so she was able to perform in the back line. Then she got so good at it that they put her in the front line.

Then she traveled with the orchestra for a while, but as time went on I suppose she got tired of traveling, so she settled down in New York City while my father was on the road and opened a dance studio. She had a lady friend—one of the original members of the chorus—who worked with her.

My mother was the financial wiz behind my father. He had more formal education than my mother—she only had two years of college—but she was a wizard with figures. He would make the money, and she would save it. And then he would spend it. But she would always make sure she saved a portion of it. Without her he would have been in a fix a long time ago. When she died, naturally he was broken up by her loss, but then he was also broken up at not having her there to maintain the everyday functions, such as taking care of business, because he had no idea where to begin. She took care of everything, and everything ran smoothly. She ran the house, took care of all the affairs and any kind of legal problems. This was a pretty big loss to him.

After my mother died he started to go back on the road. He went to France—I believe it was in 1974—to play the jazz festival in Nice. Dickie Wells was over there, and Eubie Blake did the concert, but because of his age he couldn't fulfill the full length of the stay, which was three or four weeks, so my father played the main concert and then continued traveling throughout Europe. He went to Germany, France, and Switzerland, and I guess it really took his mind off things and he really enjoyed it.

Just before the European trip his first granddaughter was born. Her name is Shereen, and she is now fifteen. She really filled a void in his life. I mean, he was really crazy about her. It's unfortunate that he couldn't stay around long enough to see her blossom into a young lady. But he really enjoyed being with her. My wife and I and the baby sometimes used to travel to meet him at out-of-town places, and it would just light up his eyes to see his granddaughter. I think this helped him maintain his sanity.

He played a club in Syracuse, the Dinkler Motor Inn, and we used to go up there and meet him. He had a few friends in Syracuse, and he was gradually getting over his loss. It took quite a while. But my father could put on a big front. I guess being in show business as long as he was, he developed the surface pretense of everything being okay, even when it wasn't. As I said earlier, he never did really express his emotions.

Master of Jazz

Like many musicians, Claude Hopkins was multitalented. A number of musicians are good athletes, others have attained a degree of expertise as artists—Pee Wee Russell and Bob Haggart come to mind—and not a few have turned out worthwhile books. Claude's hobby was woodworking, an interest he shared (although neither one was aware of it) with Pee Wee Erwin. Claude Jr. put it this way:

My father was a master carpenter. I'm sure that if he didn't have his talent for music he could have been a ship builder, or he could have been a builder of any structure he wanted to. He could take a piece of scrap wood and make a beautiful table out of it, or a cabinet. I mean, he was really sharp in the workshop, and this was something he enjoyed doing.

He had his woodworking shop in the basement, and he really enjoyed going down to the shop. You could hear the saws buzzing and the drills humming, and it might be eleven or one o'clock at night, and he couldn't sleep. He might be working on a song and was hitting a stumbling block or something, so he would go down to the shop and do a little woodworking.

I remember one of the many sacrifices he made for me when I was a kid. I think it was my seventh or eighth Christmas, and I wanted a train set. Well, the only place where he could set the train set up was in the room where he had his workshop. He took his workshop apart—took all the tools and everything out and put them in another storage area—so he could set the trains up for me. As a kid I didn't appreciate what he did, but when I got older I appreciated it even more.

The layout he made took up the whole room. He had tunnels, and towns he built by hand, and a farm area that he constructed, with little farm animals, and there were little people. It was really a beautiful setup. And I know now that it must have meant a lot to him, for him to give up something he enjoyed so much for me. As a kid you don't realize the sacrifices your parents make for you, but when you get older you learn to appreciate them.

But this was something my father always did throughout his life— make sacrifices. He wouldn't even give it a second thought. I could go to him and ask for the last dollar in his pocket, and he wouldn't say, "Well, I only have a dollar, I'll give you fifty cents." Instead, without any hesitation, he would go into his pocket and hand me the dollar. That's the way my father was.

About a year after Mabel Hopkins died, Claude began to carry on a romance with Flora Walden Chase, the widow of another pianist, Tommy Chase. Claude and Tommy had been friends from boyhood and were schoolmates. He first met Flora when the Chases came to visit at the Cotton Club, so they were already old friends. After they lost their mates, it was natural and comfortable for them to get together.

Flora said:

I really regret we did not get married, but I felt he needed more time to get his family problems—son, house, et cetera—in order. I do recall, at one of those Manassas Jazz Festivals, I had rushed to the hotel from school, it was dinner time before the concert, and when I approached the dining room everybody stood up and applauded. I was surprised and unaware of the reason, and then, I think it was either John Eaton or Tommy Gwaltney who announced, "Congratulations! Claude has just announced your wedding plans!"

Of this I knew nothing! I was even a little peeved that Claude had said nothing to me. I remember, too, that at the late party Mrs. McCree [Barbara McCree, wife of Manassas Jazz Festival producer, Johnson McCree] pleaded with me to marry him, and said how well-mated we were. I wish we had married soon after, even though Claude was too shy to propose.

Claude did keep in touch with Flora, however, with a stream of postcards and letters from various playing locations. In July 1973 he was working at the Dinkler Motor Inn, in Syracuse, New York, and he sent the following message: "If you can make Syracuse, Route 81 is a gas—great highway—you don't need any money nor a room, as I am not sleeping in the back yard. Forget the credit cards, they are no good around me."

Flora decided to accept the invitation but took a plane instead of making the long drive, and Claude met her at the airport. The flight arrived around 5 P.M., but Claude admitted he had been waiting since 11 A.M., saying, "I didn't want to miss you."

"It was really a fun trip," Flora recalled:

Russell "Big Chief" Moore was sharing the billing at the Dinkler. I knew him from the time he had worked Blues Alley with my husband. We did a lot of sight-seeing, as Claude had his car. One drive took us to Newark, New York, to visit Charles and Grace Jones's home [friends of Claude's]. On the way, on the expressway, Claude missed his exit, so rather than drive all the way to Rochester—the next exit—he used a "For Official Cars Only" U-turn, scaring me half to death. We made the turn, but traffic was bearing down on us, and I'm sure we were roundly cursed by some of the drivers. I had never met the Joneses but found them quite warm and friendly. They adored Claude, and we have kept a correspondence going ever since.

At the end of that month, Claude flew to California to play a concert. A brief note to Flora read: "Concord Inn Garden Hotel, Willow Pass Road and Hotel Way, Concord, CA.—Well, here I am in CA. We are about 15 miles north of San Francisco. The concert is only 3 hours—Quincy Jones, George Shearing and the Masters of Jazz (that's us)."

Claude Jr. remembered the concert: "He performed there with Quincy Jones. They had a big jazz concert. Quincy Jones did a little dialogue about him and really spoke a nice piece."

A year later Hopkins made his first trip to the Nice Jazz Festival. In a long letter dated July 18, 1974, he described his reactions to Flora:

> Frantel Nice
> 28, Ave. Notre-Dame
> 06000 Nice
>
> I am enclosing a program of the festival so you will understand what is really happening. The food situation is critical in that you can't eat when you want to, only when they say. Impossible to get anything done between 12 noon and 2:30 PM. Everything stops—stores close, banks close, buses stop running, restaurants won't serve. How about that? I fly to Switzerland Saturday, and fly right back to Nice Sunday. Then next week I go to Italy and Spain for that week. I recorded (trio) Wednesday, July 17, and I think it turned out pretty good. He will send me an album to the states when they are ready. Things are so expensive in this city, because it is a resort for the rich. Rooms at the beachfront hotels start at $75.00 per day, up to $450.00 a day. Out of sight.

In October he was back in Syracuse at the Dinkler, and apparently all was going well. "The group had a fantastic opening," he wrote. "The boss is smiling all over the joint and the agent is really happy. That should mean some good work for the group. Tommy [Gwaltney] is really happy. The group really sounds good and Van Perry is upsetting everybody with his singing."

He repeated the date at the Dinkler in May 1975, and in October reported:

Johnson McCree called me today concerning the Manassas Festival, which is to be Dec. 6–8. I OK'd the deal. I haven't told you I received a letter from Zurich and the promoter will be here this month. He has 20 or more concerts for me plus some recordings. I wouldn't like to go over during the winter months. It will be sometime in May. Do you think you will be able to go? Zurich is in Switzerland and there will be the Scandinavian countries also. I have been working at Jimmy Ryan's and in Fairfield, Conn. since I've been home from Syracuse.

By now the pattern was well set, and Claude was making out very well as a freelancer, much in demand at festivals, and always welcome in the clubs. In November 1976 he wrote Flora with obvious elation: "The cruise starts Feb. 7 and they fly us to New Orleans as the trip starts from there. We first go to Mexico and the Caribbean. This is the highlight of my career, I think. The money is out of sight."

And once again from the Dinkler in June 1977, he happily reported: "I start with Woody Allen when I get back home for the summer. I go back to Boston in the fall at the Berklee School of Music. Eddie Barefield [saxophonist and arranger] is here and says hello."

Claude Hopkins never stopped playing, and although long stints at Mahogany Hall and the Nevele took him out of the public eye, they also provided a good living and enabled him to maintain his skills at the keyboard. His return to freelancing around New York City coincided rather neatly with the revival of interest in the 1970s in jazz and jazz musicians and brought renewed appreciation of Claude's piano artistry, especially from other jazz musicians, who never hesitated to hire him. It was during this period that Claude and I worked together.

In keeping with Claude's latter-day recognition as a jazz pianist, evidenced by the increasing demand for his services at concerts and festivals, was the revised interest in his recordings. Through the late 1960s and into the 1970s, LPs were issued that not only recapped the records issued in the 1930s, but also for the first time made available unreleased sides and transcription dates. In addition, he was back in the studios in person, and to those with ears willing to listen, he was somewhat of a revelation.

In his liner notes for the Chiaroscuro recording, *Crazy Fingers,* the Hopkins solo album made in 1973, Stanley Dance had some pertinent observations:

A talent is revealed here which none of the early band recordings could have *entirely* prepared the listener for, although they did rather more than offer hints. The infamous pianos on which Hopkins was often heard around New York during the '50s and '60s certainly tended to obscure it, and his touch, sensitivity and lyricism were never really appropriate to Dixieland contexts. Here he emerges as the greatest living exponent— along with The Lion [Willie Smith]—of the "stride" idiom, and it is not surprising that he should name James P. Johnson and Fats Waller as primary sources of inspiration.

Perhaps Fred Norman said it best: "I have heard critics say that Claude Hopkins wasn't really a great pianist—not in the same class as Earl Hines or Art Tatum, for instance. Well, this is a matter of opinion, but if they are in the first team, then Claude has to be number one in the second team."

Crazy Fingers

Claude Hopkins Remembered

Claude Hopkins's old friend, Fred Norman, spoke of Claude's last days:

The last time I saw Claude his health was failing and he had become kind of a recluse. I went to his house one day to visit him, and his daughter-in-law said, "Just stand here at the door a minute and I'll see if he wants to see you." She went inside, and after she came back she said, "He's not well, and he doesn't want to see anyone."

So that was the last time. I really didn't get to see him even then, but my wife told me that maybe a year before he died she saw him walking up Amsterdam Avenue. She was on a bus and couldn't get his attention.

But I attended his funeral. That is, I went to the funeral parlor, and I met his son, who has grown into a wonderful young man. Claude never got his due publicity wise, because he had one of the leading bands of the swing era. I'll always remember him, and I think of him very often.

Like many of Claude's friends, Cork O'Keefe was also unable to get in touch with him:

One of the things that broke my heart was that during the last year the man was alive I could never, much as I tried, get his telephone number. I had heard he wasn't well, and the people who were taking care of him did a good job, but they kept him in hiding, instead of letting him see some of his friends. I had been pretty good friends with him. I understand his son took care of him, but it broke my heart, because I would say to a lot of the guys, "Where the hell is Claude?" But I couldn't get to see the guy.

It was a tragic situation, but only Claude Jr. knew how tragic. His recollections of his father's final years are full of deep-seated love and sadness. One has to read between the lines to appreciate the depth of feeling and the day-to-day agony the entire Hopkins family lived with for the years of Claude's lingering decline before his death on February 22, 1984.

By the time his second grandchild (his first grandson) was born, his health was already failing. Jevin, now seven, was born in the Bronx in 1980. My father's health started to fail in 1979. He went over to play a concert in Europe and got sick. I think it all started when he was playing somewhere and on the way home he slipped on some ice and fell, hitting his head on the ice. I don't know for certain if one thing has anything to do with the other, but he wasn't ever quite right afterwards. He started to have complaints. He went to a couple of doctors and they treated him with medication. This was when he was getting ready for the trip to Denmark. Then he went to Denmark and he got really ill, and they had to cancel his engagement.

They put him on a plane and sent him home. When I got the phone call about my father I had no idea where he was coming in from. All I knew from the phone call was that they were putting him on a plane. I'm at the airport looking for him, not knowing what flight he was coming in on, or what country he was coming from, because he had been traveling around Europe. And I never did meet him at the airport. He came in at one end while I was waiting at the other. So after waiting there for over ten hours I returned home, and to my surprise found him sitting in his room. It was almost as if he had just come from around the corner.

I know he realized he had just come back from Europe, but I noticed that his mental state was not great. He seemed confused. And from that point on he seemed to deteriorate. I don't believe that after that concert he ever performed again professionally. They tried to get him to play a couple of concerts—a couple of gigs in the city—and he may have played one or two, but that was it.

Around 1979 I had to put him in the hospital. His kidneys had failed. They put him on dialysis, and he was in the hospital for about four months. He was also regressing mentally, and sometimes didn't know where he was. At times he didn't know what day it was, and he had to go for dialysis three times a week. I brought him home, but he was just getting worse. I had to watch him like I did my daughter. He just seemed to give up. He wouldn't play the piano—wouldn't even touch it. And he had a couple of seizures, so I had to rush him back to the hospital.

For the next four years it was a pretty rough time. He went through some financial troubles due to his illness, and I was trying to take care of him and run my life and my family, and it was beginning to take its toll. So we sold the house in Manhattan (Washington Heights), and I bought a co-op in the Bronx. We moved my father to the Bronx with us, and I took care of him for the next three years. But he continued to regress. He got so bad I couldn't get him out of his room, and I couldn't leave him in the house alone. It was difficult to get some kind of assistance like a nurse to come in and take care of him, so I had to make a decision—

the only decision left to make, but a pretty difficult one—he had to go into a nursing home. Until this day that decision hurts me, but as I knew his condition, and since the doctors told me I was doing him a disservice by not putting him in a home where he could get the care he needed, I searched around and located one.

It was a fairly good home located in Riverdale, and it kind of eased my mind a little, knowing that it was. It was the Parkview Nursing Home, and they gave my father good care. I would go and take him out—take him for a drive. He called the home a hotel, and he thought he was in a hotel. Every time I went to see him, when the visit was over I could see the hurt in his eyes when I left. He was like the kid you leave on your doorstep when you go to work, and you can see the kid looking at you sadly without saying anything.

They tried to get my father to play the piano while he was in the home, but he wouldn't. He was a very stubborn man, once his mind was set on something. He lived in the home for a couple of years.

When I moved from the Bronx to New Jersey I wasn't able to visit him as often as before because of the distance involved, and that really bothered me. I don't know if that affected my father's mental state even more, but one night I got a call from the doctor stating that he had expired. The doctor said that he left this world in a peaceful state. I was happy to hear that he left peacefully and that he is somewhere in Heaven playing the golden harp, or playing the eighty-eight keys, and looking down on us.

One thing I can firmly say is that my father enjoyed his life while he was here. He was eighty-one when he died. And he really had a lot of fun, so he had no reason to look back and say, "I wish I had done that, or I wish I had done this." He did it! He was not a perfect man, but what man is? He took care of his family, and he never abused me or my mother. He was a very caring person.

Appendix A

Chronology of
Claude Hopkins's Career

1920–24
Local gigs around Washington, D.C., climaxed with the job at the Oriental Gardens.

1925
Hired by Herndon Daniels for Atlantic City engagement, which folded. By luck manages to get work at Smile Awhile Cafe in Asbury Park, which leads to booking for European tour with the *Revue Nègre*. Show sails for France on Sept. 21.

1926
Revue Nègre closes in Berlin on March 2, 1926. Claude puts together international band and tours Europe for rest of the year and into 1927.

1927
Claude and Mabel sail for home on March 27. Organizes band to play Club Bohemia, followed by Atlantic City date and return to Smile Awhile Cafe until Labor Day. Went to New York, and band disbands. Claude takes rent-party gigs and subs for Luckey Roberts. In the fall attends rehearsals of Ginger Snaps of 1928 and joins show to tour.

1928
Mostly devoted to tour of Ginger Snaps of 1928. Balance of the year at Fulton Gardens, in Brooklyn, until it closes in 1929.

1929
Claude takes a job as a piano player in dancing school and winds up taking over the band and arranging audition with Joe Ward for job at Cocoanut Grove. This, in turn, leads to Savoy Ballroom.

1930–31
Band at Savoy Ballroom. Claude augments at suggestion of management and adds two trumpets (Sylvester Lewis and Ovie Alston) and one trombone (Nelson Hurd).

1932
Band moves to Roseland Ballroom and is instant hit. Option is picked up, and group settles in for a long run. Rockwell-O'Keefe takes over as agent. Claude hires Orlando Robeson. Band makes first tour.

1933
Band at Roseland for entire year and into 1934. Fred Norman joins on second trombone and as arranger.

1934
Summer tour for Schribman brothers in New England, followed by a tour of the South. Rockwell-O'Keefe and Lew Brecker arrange for the band to open with new show at the Cotton Club.

1935
Uninterrupted residence at the Cotton Club.

1936
Canadian tour, followed by swings to Midwest and West Coast.

1937–40
Successive road tours. Band falls apart latter part of 1940.

1940–43
Claude tries arranging for other bands. Takes job in defense plant.

1944
Organizes band to play Club Zanzibar, at 49th and Broadway. Stays until club closes in 1947. Puts together small group, which records for Rainbow Records. Tours into 1949. Plays USO circuit.

1950–51
Tours with the Zanzibar Revue. Organizes another small group to play Sheraton hotels.

1951–53
Joins jazz group playing the Mahogany Hall, in Boston.

1954–60
With various groups working the Metropole Cafe in New York.

1960–66
Plays with trio at the Nevele in the Catskills.

1967–69
With the Jazz Giants.

1970–79
Freelances. Plays Nice Festival, tours Europe.

Appendix B

Comments, Criticisms, and Corrections

In the biography *Duke Ellington*, Barry Ulanov briefly mentions Claude Hopkins in a vivid description of the early years in Washington, growing up in the same generation as Duke Ellington, Otto Hardwick, the Miller brothers, and other budding musicians:

The atmosphere was softly, insinuatingly urban; the architecture, mixed ante-bellum South and pre-Christian Greece, imposed a certain dignity upon those colored youngsters which no other group of jazzmen—those from New Orleans, Chicago, Kansas City or New York, to name the principal sources of jazz talent—ever possessed. Duke had it, of course, so had Otto Hardwick, the Miller brothers, Bill Escoffery, Claude Hopkins, Arthur Whetsol, Elmer Snowden, Rex Stewart, all the musicians who were born or bred in the capital; they had it, they have it. There was a Washington pattern; it involved a certain bearing, a respect for education, for the broad principles of the art of music, a desire for order, for design, in their professional lives.

These men comprised an exceptional group, and almost to a man they went on to become distinguished musicians, and the polish and dignity Ulanov describes stayed with Claude for the rest of his life. As Cork O'Keefe stated with emphasis, "Claude was a gentleman!"

Ulanov also wrote: "Claude, a neighbor, was making some headway as a bandleader and pianist, too, with occasional jobs in New York and offers from Europe and Australia."

The "occasional jobs in New York" is verified to some extent. Brian Rust, in his *Jazz Records 1897–1942*, lists Claude, along with Arthur Whetsol and Elmer Snowden, as accompanying blues singer Sara Martin on a record date for Columbia in November 1922, and in *The World of Swing*, by Stanley Dance, Claude talks about working with Wilbur Sweatman. On the other hand, it's doubtful if, at this early stage, he was getting offers from Europe and Australia because he doesn't mention it in his journal.

John Chilton, in *Who's Who in Jazz*, states that the Hopkins band played in Atlantic City in 1924 and sailed for Europe in September 1925. The Hopkins journal clearly shows that both dates should be 1925. Chilton also fails to mention Asbury Park and the Smile Awhile Cafe, where Claude's career as a bandleader actually took off, and omits *Barbershop Blues* in the brief Hopkins biography.

The Cotton Club, by Jim Haskins, a history of the famous nightspot, overlooks the two years (November 1934 to New Year's Eve 1936) that the Hopkins band played there. This neglect has been compounded in the later volume, *The Guinness Jazz A–Z*, compiled by editor-writers Peter Clayton and Peter Gammond, who obviously used *The Cotton Club* as reference material and thus passes on the erroneous information that Jimmie Lunceford followed Cab Calloway into the club in 1934.

In *Jazz In the Movies*, David Meeker includes both movies in which the Hopkins band was featured, *Dance Team* and *Wayward*, along with the two Vitaphone shorts, *Barber Shop Blues* (1933) and *By Request* (1935), but Roger Kinkle fails to list any of these films in his biography of Claude Hopkins in *The Complete Encyclopedia of Popular Music and Jazz, 1900–1950*.

In *The Swing Era*, Gunther Schuller is guilty of several inaccuracies. For example, on page 318, he writes of "a splendidly played trumpet trio, one of the trademarks of the Hopkins band from its Alston-led days." In his journal, Claude relates taking over the dancing school band formerly led by pianist Charlie Skeets, and the lone trumpet player was Elmer Edwards. Only after the band was booked into the Savoy Ballroom and Claude hired Ovie Alston and Sylvester Lewis did the band have three trumpets, and at no point in the band's history was Ovie Alston the leader, even though, for some reason, the band recorded for Bluebird under his name.

Again, on page 320, Schuller states:

A third problem was Hopkins's stride-piano style which, of course, had to be prominently featured. It was vigorous and incisive, with a strong left hand, but ultimately anachronistic. It soon became an anchor which prevented the band from veering far from its conservative moorings.

Its commercial success derived, as with almost all 1930's bands, from its singers, particularly Orlando Roberson [sic], a falsetto crooner of some skill. But then Hopkins also had Alston, a pseudo-Armstrong-style singer, and Fred Norman, who in a lugubrious halting voice talked his way through depressingly sad though lightweight story-telling pieces, which were a flagrant plagiarism of Don Redman's novelty-hokum approach—except that Redman had a light, high, almost childish voice whereas Norman's was low and oafish.

Contrary to Mr. Schuller's contention that the band's popularity stemmed from its singers, it was the "vigorous and incisive" Hopkins piano style, along with the band's soft but infectious rhythmic approach, that propelled the band to its initial success. The band was already a featured radio presentation before Claude hired Orlando Robeson as an added commercial attraction. As for characterizing the Hopkins stride piano style as "anachronistic" and preventing the band from "veering from its conservative moorings," the question comes to mind: In relation to what? Are we to automatically assume that all proponents of the stride style are out of date? If so, we must disregard a number of prestigious names in jazz history—James P. Johnson, Fats Waller, Willie "The Lion" Smith, Dick Wellstood, Dick Hyman, Ralph Sutton—just to mention a few of the better-known practitioners. Why are we to accept the opinion that the Hopkins band was "conservative" in its approach? How does this conform with Claude's refusal to let the band open up and blast at the Savoy, even though he was taking a chance of displeasing the management? The Hopkins band had its own style, recognizably different from that of its contemporaries, but does that mean they were conservative, or were they simply daring to be original?

Schuller isn't kind to the vocalists either, even though he does contend they were the reason for the band's success. His gratuitous depictions of Robeson as a "falsetto crooner of some skill" and Ovie Alston as a "pseudo-Armstrong-style singer" are dubious at best, but in Fred Norman's case he is completely off base. By stating that Norman's efforts were "a flagrant plagiarism" of Don Redman, he opens himself to criticism for not recognizing that the true root of the vocals was the work of the great black comedian Bert Williams, who starred in vaudeville and musical shows early in the century and was featured in a number of Ziegfeld's "Follies," beginning in 1910. Norman's vocals are direct derivatives of Williams's famous monologues of "Nobody," "Woodsman, Spare That Tree," "The Darktown Poker Club," and similar original novelties. The Williams "patter" style was much admired and imitated. Fred Norman was not the first nor the last, as Phil Harris demonstrated many years later.

Schuller does allocate some kind words to the soloists, but for the most part his assessment of the Hopkins band's musical worth is heavily based on the phonograph records it made, as evaluated almost half a century later. He fails to take into consideration that the band didn't record until 1932, and by that time it was already a successful radio attraction, firmly established at Roseland, and up to that time the only vocalist was Ovie Alston.

Still later in his analysis he attributes the band's breakup to a "trend of deterioration. . . . Its Swing having long ago become overly polite, its repertory flirting with classical propriety (misunderstood at that), its style hardened into colorless redundancies, it faded away—and disbanded in 1942—even before the big band breakups of 1946 and 1948."

As a matter of fact, according to an item in *Down Beat* dated May 1, 1941, Claude Hopkins filed for bankruptcy in that year. And Mr. Schuller's contention that the big years for the band breakups were 1946 and 1948 indicates he isn't familiar with the events of 1942, when the country was feeling the pinch of "defense" measures—strict rationing of such necessities to road bands as gasoline, tires, food, automobiles—not to mention the deadly depredations into the ranks of musicians by a phenomenon of the times called the draft. The years 1942 and 1943 were critical in the band business and saw the demise of hundreds of dance bands, the majority of which were never reorganized after the war. Nothing dealt a heavier blow to the bands than World War II, and most of them were long gone before 1946 or 1948.

Furthermore, by 1941 and 1942 the business was rife with bands playing "colorless redundancies," and the trend was by no means confined to any one band—especially that of Claude Hopkins. It only requires a bit of listening to the contemporary recordings to prove this.

More than likely, other factors were the real reasons Claude had to disband. Although he and probably all others concerned were elated when the band was tagged to move into the Cotton Club for a two-year stint, during which time it was heard on the air frequently and made no road tours, it's possible this was the beginning of the band's downhill slide. Of course, at the time nobody could have foreseen this. The radio exposure built up a ready market for the road tours that began in 1936, and for a couple of years the bookings were plentiful and profitable under the Rockwell-O'Keefe office. But the Cotton Club engagement turned out to be the last location spot of any duration or prestige, and from that time forward the band was constantly on the road.

This is verified by the band listings in *Down Beat* and *Metronome* for the years 1936 through 1940, which designate the Hopkins unit as "on tour" without a break. It's very likely that after a while the constant touring had the negative result of taking the band out of the public eye, and the public has an infamous reputation for a short memory. Out of sight, out of mind.

Claude Hopkins parted company with Rockwell-O'Keefe in 1937 and went with the William Morris Agency, only to change again to Harold Oxley in 1940. He doesn't explain why he made the changes, but the most obvious guess would be a fall-off in bookings.

Another factor is worth consideration. The fantastic success of the Benny Goodman band propelled swing into the forefront of popular music, with the result that all at once the market was cluttered with bands competing in a field that only a short time before had been almost the exclusive property of the black bands. Jazz was no longer a monopoly, and the "hot" white bands had the choice of the best locations.

Just one more comment: Schuller describes the Hopkins band's popularity as "relatively short-lived." It actually lasted for ten years, and with a comparatively small turnover in personnel. In the precarious era of the big bands, that was pretty remarkable.

Over a span of half a century or more, some memory lapses are understandable and excusable, such as a few discrepancies between the chronology of events as notated in Claude's journal and the way he remembered them in *The World of Swing*.

In his journal he is positive about the date he and Mabel embarked for the return trip to the States: March 27, 1927. He then writes that after a short vacation he organized a little band to play the Club Bohemia, on 11th and U streets in Washington, and in the group he had Doc Clarke on trumpet; Sandy Williams, trombone; Bernie Addison, guitar; Bob Brown, drums; Hilton Jefferson, alto; and Elmer Williams, tenor. Allowing a couple of weeks for the rest period after the strenuous European tour and ocean crossing, we can safely assume this was around April, or possibly into May. Next he relates that from the Club Bohemia he took the band back to the Smile Awhile Cafe in Asbury Park for the summer of 1927, and after Labor Day the band—with the exception of Doc Clarke and Bob Brown—went to New York to try its luck and disbanded when no work was available. Then he "hung around" taking rent-party gigs and whatever else came along.

In *The World of Swing*, he says that his first job after the return from Paris was at the Smile Awhile Cafe. No mention is made of the Club Bohemia. He continues: "Then I bought a touring car, and took a band and a girl singer to work for Herman [sic] Daniels at the Belmont on North Carolina Avenue in Atlantic City. . . . That's where I had Elmer Snowden on banjo, Artie 'Schiefe' Whetsol (who later went with Duke) on trumpet, Bass Hill, and a drummer."

There seem to be a number of slips here that can only be straightened out by putting them in logical sequence, backed up by what we know to be facts. Since Claude is so definite about it in his journal, we can safely assume the Club Bohemia job took place, but it may have been of short duration, possibly only a couple of weeks. Now, in his liner notes for *Crazy Fingers* (Chiaroscuro 114), Stanley Dance wrote: "The band, moreover, had a distinctive character, which Hopkins deliberately maintained for a long time. Trombonist Sandy Williams has recalled that, when he played with him as early as 1927 in Atlantic City, Hopkins was already emphasizing softness in his music."

Unfortunately, Hopkins didn't mention Sandy Williams as part of the band in Atlantic City, but it appears the trombonist was in it, and his reference to 1927 is on target. However, Claude's statement that his first date was the Smile Awhile Cafe has to be wrong, and after the Club Bohemia he took the group he mentions to Atlantic City for another stay, which couldn't have lasted very long, and this, in turn, was followed by the return to the Smile Awhile Cafe until Labor Day.

In his narrative in *The World of Swing*, Claude goes on to compound the mix-up. He completely eliminates all reference to his rent-party period in the fall of 1927, and the association with Luckey Roberts, and relates: "Then I went to New York and worked at a dancing school on Eighth Avenue and 57th Street. The band was Charlie Skeete's [sic] and he had a boy named Edwards on trumpet, Pete Jacobs on drums, a bass, and a couple of saxes. I began to write for this group, and it soon became a little different from the average dancing school band, and they suggested I take it over. . . . After that, for about a year I went out on tour with the Ginger Snaps Revue, playing the colored T.O.B.A. circuit."

The impression here is that Claude traveled to New York right after the Atlantic City job to play the dancing school, and then followed this by touring with the Ginger Snaps Revue, which in his journal is named Ginger Snaps of 1928, and began rehearsing late in 1927. Actually, 1928 was mainly devoted to the Ginger Snaps tour until the show went broke, and the balance of 1928 and part of 1929 to working in the Brooklyn club, the Fulton Gardens.

After the Fulton Gardens closed in 1929, Claude states, "I got a job in a dancing school called Venetian Gardens, on 8th Avenue and 57th Street as just a piano player. . . . I began talking to the men in the band who had been there a long time about forming a band (legitimate), and getting a better job. This group was comprised of Edmond Hall (sax & cl), Bobby Sands (tenor), Pete Jacobs (drums), Henry Turner (bass), Elmer Edwards (trumpet), and Walter 'Joe' Jones, guitar. The group was originally headed by pianist Charlie Skeets, whom I replaced."

Hopkins goes on to mention the audition for Joe Ward, which resulted in the job at the club under the Apollo Theater he called the Grotto in the journal and the Cocoanut Grove in *The World of Swing*, and this led to the booking in the Savoy Ballroom.

In his journal Claude wrote, "I stayed at the club from 1944 to 1947, until it closed." The club he is referring to was the Club Zanzibar, at Broadway and 49th Street. In Claude's handwriting, a notation in red ink in the margin of the journal, where he begins to write about the Zanzibar, reads "1944."

John Chilton, in *Who's Who in Jazz*, in his biographical sketch of Claude Hopkins, tells us: "From 1937 to 1940 did extensive touring, occasional residencies in New York, etc. Reorganized band in 1941, played on West Coast, New York, etc., until disbanding in 1942. In 1943 worked as an inspector at the Eastern Aircraft factory in New Jersey and led the company's Wild Cat Band. Also led own band on tour of Canada, Ohio, etc. (September–November 1943). In October 1944 formed new band for residency at Club Broadway, New York, etc., early in 1946 own big band into Zanzibar, New York."

Without saying so Chilton infers that the band broke up sometime in 1940, and Claude reorganized in 1941, disbanding again in 1942. This isn't likely, and Claude's journal makes no mention of reorganizing after the 1940 breakup. The West Coast tour alluded to is probably the one made by the band just before the breakup. The Canadian tour took place right after it left the Cotton Club, certainly not while Claude was at Eastern Aircraft.

Here's what Claude had to say in *The World of Swing*, as quoted by Stanley Dance: "I formed an entertaining troupe to play in a lot of Sheraton Hotel cocktail lounges. . . . We made a couple of records with this group. There was quite a bit of singing, and I even sang myself. That lasted until 1941, when Joe Howard called me. 'Hop, can you get a band together in two weeks and open up at the Zanzibar? . . .' And I was there until '44."

Neither in his journal or in the interview for Dance does Claude mention a Club Broadway. The journal is quite definite in dating the Club Zanzibar engagement as beginning in 1944.

Appendix C

Filmography

The Claude Hopkins Orchestra appeared in the following movie shorts and features.

1931
Dance Team. Fox Film Corporation. Feature film starring Paul Lucas and Irene Dunn. 83 minutes.

1932
Wayward. Feature film starring Richard Arlen and Nancy Carroll. 76 minutes.

1933
Barber Shop Blues. Vitaphone short. With four Stepp Brothers and vocalists. "Trees," "St. Louis Blues," "Nagasaki," and "Loveless Love." Personnel: Albert Snaer, Sylvester Lewis, Ovie Alston, trumpets; Fernando Arbello, Fred Norman, trombones; Gene Johnson, Edmond Hall, Bobby Sands, reeds; Claude Hopkins, piano; Walter Joe Jones, guitar; Henry Turner, bass, tuba; Pete Jacobs, drums; Orlando Robeson, vocals. 9 minutes.

1935

Broadway Highlights. Paramount short. Shows Claude Hopkins Orchestra rehearsing at the Cotton Club. Nina Mae McKinney and Cora LeRedd are featured. 10 minutes.

By Request. Vitaphone short. With Tip, Tap, and Toe. "I Would Do Anything for You," "Chasing My Blues Away," "California, Here I Come," "To Call You My Own," "Shine," "Chinatown, My Chinatown." Personnel: Albert Snaer, Sylvester Lewis, Ovie Alston, trumpets; Henry Wells, Fred Norman, trombones; Gene Johnson, Edmond Hall, Hilton Jefferson, Bobby Sands, reeds; Claude Hopkins, piano; Walter Joe Jones, guitar; Henry Turner, bass; Pete Jacobs, drums; Orlando Robeson, vocals. 10 minutes.

Appendix D

Discography

Key to abbreviations: ARC, American Record Corporation; Br, Brunswick; Col, Columbia; CBS, Columbia Broadcasting System; Dec, Decca; DL, Decca LP; Par, Parlophone; Voc, Vocalion.

Sarah Martin

New York, November 18, 1922

Accompanied by her Brown Skin Syncopaters: Arthur Whetsol, trumpet; Claude Hopkins, piano; Elmer Snowden, banjo.

80678-1-2 "I Loved You Once but You   Col rejected
       Stayed Away Too Long"
80679-1-2 " 'Tain't Nobody's Biz-ness If   Col rejected
       I Do"

Clarence Williams' Washboard Five

New York, September 20, 1928

Ed Allen, cornet; Arville Harris, clarinet, alto; Claude Hopkins, piano; Floyd Casey, washboard; Ben Waters, clarinet, tenor; Clarence Williams, vocals and possibly second piano, last chorus each side.

401152-A "Walk That Broad"

401153-A "Have You Ever Felt That Way?"

Okeh 8629, Voc 03350, Jazz Unlimited 4

Voc 03350 as *Clarence Williams and His Orchestra*, Matrix 19936-1

Appendix D

Claude Hopkins and His Orchestra

New York, May 24, 1932

Albert Snaer, Sylvester Lewis, Ovie Alston, trumpets; Fernando Arbello, trombone; Edmond Hall, clarinet, alto, baritone; Gene Johnson, alto; Bobby Sands, tenor; Claude Hopkins, piano arranger; Walter "Joe" Jones, guitar; Henry Turner, tuba; Pete Jacobs, drums; Orlando Robeson, vocals; Jimmy Mundy, arranger.

152199-1 "I Would Do Anything for You"

Col 2655-D, GAPS 120

152200-1 "Mad Moments" (Claude Hopkins, arranger)

Col 2655-D, GAPS 120

152201-1 "Mush Mouth" (Jimmy Mundy, arranger)

Col 2674-D, GAPS 120

152202-1 "How'm I Doin'" (Orlando Robeson, vocals)

Col 2674-D, GAPS 120

New York, May 25, 1932

11893-A "Three Little Words" (Claude Hopkins, arranger)

Jazz Archives JA-4

11894-A "I Would Do Anything for You" (Orlando Robeson, vocals)

Jazz Archives JA-4

11895-A "Hopkins' Scream"

Jazz Archives JA-4

11896-A "Washington Squabble"

Jazz Archives JA-4

(Above tracks from unissued ARC masters.)

New York, January 13, 1933

152351-2 "Look Who's Here"

Col 2741-D, DO-890

152352-2 "He's a Son of the South" (Ovie Alston, vocals)

Col 2747-D, DO-896, Par R-15

152353-1 "Canadian Capers"

Col 2747-D, DO-896, Par R-15

152354-1 "California Here I Come"

Col 2741-D, DO-890, Par R-208, MC-3019

152355-1 "I've Got the World on a   Rejected
        String"

New York, March 9, 1933

13129-A "Three Little Words"   Jazz Archives JA-4
13132-A "Shake Your Ashes"   Jazz Archives JA-4
13131-A "Mystic Moan"   Jazz Archives JA-4
13132-A "Just You, Just Me" (Orlando   Jazz Archives JA-4   *Discography*
        Robeson, vocals)
13133-A "Washington Squabble"   Jazz Archives JA-4
13134-A "Ain't Misbehavin' " (Orlando Jazz Archives JA-4
        Robeson, vocals)
13135-A "Honeysuckle Rose"   Jazz Archives JA-4

(Above tracks from unissued Brunswick masters.)

New York, 1933

Albert Snaer, Sylvester Lewis, Ovie Alston, trumpets; Fernando Arbello, Fred Norman, trombones; Edmond Hall, cornet, alto, baritone; Gene Johnson, alto, clarinet; Bobby Sands, tenor; Claude Hopkins, piano; Walter Jones, guitar; Henry Turner, bass; Pete Jacobs, drums.

"Loveless Love"   Extreme Rarities LP1004,
                                   Cicala (It)BLJ8009,
                                   Bandstand BS7127

(From Vitaphone short, *Barbershop Blues;* entire soundtrack on Harlequin HQ2038.)

New York, December 11, 1933

Henry Turner played only string bass from this point; Fred Norman, trombone; vocals, arrangements added.

B-14437-A "Washington Squabble"   Br 6750, 01779, A-
                                   500375; GAPS 120
B-14438-A "Mystic Moan"   Br 6750, 01779, A-
                                   500375; GAPS 120

New York, January 11, 1934

152666-2 "Marie" (Orlando Robeson,   Col 2904-D; Par R-1815,
        vocals)   A-3933; GAPS 120
152667-2 "Ain't Misbehavin"   Col 2880-D; Par R-2134,
                                     A-3838; GAPS 120

152668-2 "Harlem Rhythm Dance"	Col 2880-D, Par R-2283, A-3838
152669-2 "Minor Mania"	Col 2904-D, DB-5019; Par A-3933, GAPS 120, Milan 252/3

New York, April 6, 1934

15043-A "My Gal Sal" (Orlando Robeson, vocals)	Jazum 46
15044-A "Three Little Words" (Claude Hopkins, arranger)	CBS 88134

New York, May 3, 1934

15161-A "Everybody Shuffle" (Ovie Alston, vocals)	Br 6916
15162-A "Don't Let Your Love Go Wrong" (Ovie Alston, vocals)	Br 6891
15163-A "I Can't Dance (I Got Ants in My Pants)" (Fred Norman, vocals, with ensemble)	Br 6916
15164-A "Margie" (Orlando Robeson, vocals)	Br 6916

New York, September 14, 1934

38669-A "Chasing All the Blues Away" (Ovie Alston, vocals)	Dec 441; Br 01941, A-9904, A-825
38670-A "Just You, Just Me" (Orlando Robeson, vocals)	Dec 185; Br 01941, A-9904, A-825
38671-A "King Porter Stomp" (Fred Norman, arranger)	Dec 184, Br 02120, DL79242
38672-B "In the Shade of the Old Apple Tree"	Dec 184, Voc S-176, Br A-81608, Swingfan (G) 1010
38673-A "Who?" (Orlando Robeson, vocals)	Dec 185

New York, October 22, 1934

Hilton Jefferson, clarinet and alto, added.

38870-A "Walkin' the Dog" (Ovie Alston, vocals)	Dec 270, Swingfan (G) 1010
38871-A "Sweetheart o' Mine" (Orlando Robeson, vocals)	Dec 270, Swingfan (G) 1010

38872-A "Monkey Business"	Dec 674, DL 79242
38873-A "Zozoi" (Fred Norman, arranger)	Dec 674, DL 79242

New York, November 9, 1934

Snub Mosely replaced Fernando Arbello.

38986-A "Mandy" (Orlando Robeson, vocals)	Dec 353, Swingfan (G) 1010
18987-A "Do You Ever Think of Me" (Orlando Robeson, vocals)	Dec 353

New York, February 1, 1935

39320-B "Trees"	Dec 374
39321-A "Love in Bloom" (Orlando Robeson, vocals)	Dec 374
39322-A "June in January" (Orlando Robeson, vocals)	Dec 441

New York, 1935

"Chasing My Blues Away"	Jazz Anthology (F) 30 JA5156
"Lazy Bones" (Fred Norman, vocals, arranger)	Jazz Anthology (F) 30 JA5156
"Hodge Podge" (Fred Norman, arranger)	Jazz Anthology (F) 30 JA5156
"Swingin' and Jivin' " (Jimmy Mundy, arranger)	Jazz Anthology (F) 30 JA5156
"Just As Long As the World Goes 'Round" (Fred Norman, arranger)	Jazz Anthology (F) 30 JA5156
"You Stayed Away Too Long" (Ovie Alston, vocals)	Jazz Anthology (F) 30 JA5156
"Put on Your Old Grey Bonnet" (Claude Hopkins and Bob Sylvester, arrangers; Ovie Alston, vocals)	Jazz Anthology (F) 30 JA5156
"Truckin' " (Claude Hopkins and Fred Norman, arrangers)	Jazz Anthology (F) 30 JA5156
"The Preacher and the Bear" (Fred Norman, arranger)	Jazz Anthology (F) 30 JA5156
"Minor Mania" (Fred Norman, arranger)	Jazz Anthology (F) 30 JA5156
"Washington Squabble"	Jazz Anthology (F) 30 JA5156

"Farewell Blues" (Phil Lang, arranger)   Jazz Anthology (F) 30
                                            JA5156

(Above tracks also on Polydor 423269, Jazz Panorama LP 13, and Swing Classics ET2.)

New York, October 18, 1935

Singin' in the Rain. Fernando Arbello, Fred Norman, trombones; Hilton Jefferson, alto.

"I Would Do Anything for You" (theme)	Jazz Archives JA-27
"Canadian Capers"	Jazz Archives JA-27
"Nagasaki"	Milan A271
"Yankee Doodle Never Went to Town" (Ovie Alston, vocals)	Milan A271
"Backbeats"	Milan A271
"What'll I Do?"	Milan A271
"The Traffic Was Terrific" (Fred Norman, vocals)	Milan A271
"Aw, Shucks!"	Milan A271
"Singin' in the Rain"	Milan A271
"Nola"	Milan A271
"Sweet Horn" (Ovie Alston, vocals)	Milan A271
"Broadway Rhythm"	Milan A271
"Somebody" (Fred Norman, vocals)	Milan A271
"That's A-plenty"	Milan A271
"Everybody Shuffle" (Ovie Alston, vocals)	Milan A271
"In the Shade of the Old Apple Tree"	Milan A271

New York, November 1935

"Just As Long As the World Goes 'Round"	Jazzfan LP 13
"You Stayed Away Too Long" (Ovie Alston, vocals)	Jazzfan LP 13
"Put on Your Old Grey Bonnet" (Ovie Alston, vocals)	Jazzfan LP 13
"Truckin' "	Jazzfan LP 13
"The Preacher and the Bear" (Fred Norman, vocals)	Jazzfan LP 13

New York, c. November 1935

Henry Wells, trombone, replaced Fernando Arbello.

"Chasing My Blues Away" (Ovie Alston, vocals)	Jazzfan LP 13
"Lazy Bones" (Fred Norman, vocals)	Jazzfan LP 13

"Hodge Podge"	Jazzfan LP13
"Swingin' and Jivin' "	Jazzfan LP13
"Minor Mania"	Jazzfan LP13
"Washington Squabble"	Jazzfan LP13
"Farewell Blues" (Phil Lang, arranger)	Jazzfan LP13

(Also on Jazz Panorama LP13; Swing Classics ET2; Musidisc (F) 30JA5156; and, without "The Preacher and the Bear," Alamac QSR2420 and Polydor 423269.)

New York, 1935

By Request   Harlequin HQ2038

(Soundtrack for Vitaphone short. Other tracks on LP by other artists.)

New York, February 2, 1937

Shirley Clay, Jabbo Smith, Lincoln Mills, trumpets; Floyd Grady, Fred Norman, Vic Dickenson, trombones; Gene Johnson, Chauncey Haughton, Ben Smith, Bobby Sands, reeds; Claude Hopkins, piano, arranger; Walter Jones, guitar; Abe Bolar, bass; Pete Jacobs, drums; Beverly White, vocals.

61567-A	"Sunday" (Beverly White, vocals)	Dec 1153, Br 02397
61568-A-B	"No No Nora" (Beverly White, vocals)	Unissued
61569-A	"Swingin' Down the Lane"	Dec 1153, Br 02397, Swingfan (G) 1010

New York, April 21, 1937

Arville Harris, reeds, replaced Chauncey Haughton; George Forster, drums, replaced Pete Jacobs.

62140-A	"Honey" (Beverly White, vocals)	Dec 1316, Br 02464
62141-A	"June Night" (Beverly White, vocals)	Dec 1286, Br 02464
62142-A	"Church Street Sobbin' Blues"	Dec 1286, Br 02447, Br (G) 87098
62143-A	"My Kinda Love" (Beverly White, vocals)	Dec 1316, Br 02464

Ovie Alston and His Orchestra

Ovie Alston, trumpet, vocals, leader; Sylvester Lewis, Robert Cheeks, trumpets; Ray Hogan, trombone; Ben Richardson, alto, baritone; Floyd Blakemore, alto; Cliff Glover, tenor; Claude Hopkins, piano; Rudolph Williams, guitar; Abe Bolar, bass; George Forster, drums.

New York, October 14, 1938

23583-1	"Junk Man's Serenade"	Voc 4448, Col DB-5051
23584-1	"Twinkle Dinkle" (Ovie Alston, vocals)	Voc 4577, Col DB-5055, DO-19
23585-1	"Ja Da" (Ovie Alston, vocals)	Voc 4448, Col DB 5051
33586-1	"Walkin' the Dog"	Voc 4500, Col DB 5054

New York, October 21, 1938

Froshine Stewart, vocals.

23604-1	"I Let a Tear Fall in the River" (Froshine Stewart, vocals)	Voc 4462
23605-1	"Spare-Ribs and Spaghetti"	Voc 4577, Col DB-5055, DO-19
23606-1-2	"Home-Cookin' Mama" (Ovie Alston, vocals)	Voc 4500, Col DB-5054
23607-1	"How Much Do You Mean to Me?" (Ovie Alston, vocals)	Voc 4452

Carnegie Hall, New York, October 6, 1939

No known details, except unnamed female vocalist.

"I Would Do Anything for You"	Collected Classics CC18

Claude Hopkins and His Orchestra

Albert Snaer, Russell Jones, trumpets; Herman Autry, trumpet, vocals; Ray Hogan, Norman Greene, Bernard Archer, trombones; Howard Johnson, Norman Thornton, Bobby Sands, Benny Waters, reeds; Claude Hopkins, piano, arranger; Walter Jones, guitar; Elmer James, bass; Walter Johnson, drums; Orlando Robeson, vocals.

New York, February 1940

Am604	"Yacht Club Swing"	Ammor 116, Jazz Archives JA-4
Am605	"The Singing Hills" (Orlando Robeson, vocals)*	Ammor 114
Am606	"Out to Lunch"	Ammor 115
Am607	"A Little Rain Must Fall" (Orlando Robeson, vocals)	Ammor 116

| Am608 | "I'd Believe You" (Herman Autry, vocals)* | Ammor 114 | |
| Am609 | "What's the Matter with Me?" (Orlando Robeson, vocals) | Ammor 115 | *123* |

* These titles were not reissued on Jazz Archives JA-4.

Claude Hopkins Quartet

Scoville Brown, clarinet, tenor; Eddie Gibbs, guitar; John Brown, bass; Claude Hopkins, piano; Rena Collins, vocals.

New York, 1947

| "Low Gravy" | Rainbow 10035 |
| "It's Too Big Poppa" | Rainbow 10035 |

(Although the following item appeared in *Radio Daily*, if the two sides were recorded, they were never released: "Rainbow Records has a sleeper in the Rena Collins-Claude Hopkins Quartet Waxing of 'You're Gonna Be Sorry' backed with 'Baby Have You Got a Little Love to Spare?' ")

New York, August 18, 1950

Rainbow Records (?). Prince Robinson, tenor; Claude Hopkins, piano; Jimmy McLinn, guitar; John Brown, bass; George Woods, drums; Betty McLaurin, Henry Wright, Lucille Linde, Buddy Brees, vocals.

"Crying My Heart Out" (Betty McLaurin, vocals)
"Are You Forgetting Love?" (Henry Wright, vocals)
"You're Different" (Lucille Linde, vocals)
"Somebody Mentioned Your Name" (Buddy Brees, vocals)

Note: From this point on in the discography, Claude Hopkins's recordings are listed by album title.

Jazz at the Metropole

New York, 1935

Recorded live at the Metropole Cafe. Henry "Red" Allen and Charlie Shavers, trumpets; Herb Flemming, trombone; Buster Bailey, clarinet; Claude Hopkins, piano; Benny Moten, bass; Cozy Cole, drums.

"Buddy Bolden Said," "Kiss the Baby," "When the Saints Go Marching In" (Bethlehem BCP-21).

New York, 1956

Pee Wee Erwin, trumpet; Vic Dickenson, trombone; Buster Bailey, clarinet; Claude Hopkins, piano, arranger; Milt Hinton, bass; George Wettling, drums.

"The Saints," "Basin St. Blues," "Struttin' with Some Barbecue," "Clarinet Marmalade," "Royal Garden Blues," "Muskrat Ramble," "Tin Roof Blues," "I Would Do Anything for You," "Birth of the Blues" (Design DLP 38).

(Some of the foregoing material has been reissued several times, often scrambled with a later Design session featuring different musicians. International Award AK-164 and Westerfield AKS-164 are among these issues.)

Music of the Early Jazz Dances

1958

Henry Allen, Charlie Shavers, trumpets; Tyree Glenn, trombone, vibes; Vic Dickenson, trombone; Buster Bailey, clarinet; Lyle Smith, alto, clarinet; Claude Hopkins, piano; Milt Hinton, bass; Panama Francis, drums; Julia Steele, vocals.

"Alabama Walk Around," "Honolulu Dance," "When You Do the Ragtime Dance," "Scratchin' the Gravel," "When I Do the Hoochy Coochy in the Sky," "Everybody Out Tonight," "Shuffling Pete," "Walkin' the Dog," "The Pidgeoning [*sic*]," "Rules and Regulations," "Caught in the Fence," "Mississippi Side Step," "Levee Revels," "Boom E Rag," "Messin' Around," "Wiggle-Dee-Wow," "Original Black Bottom Dance" (Twentieth-Century Fox LP3009).

Claude Hopkins and His All Stars, *Yes, Indeed!*

New York, March 25, 1960

Emmett Berry, trumpet; Buddy Tate, tenor; Claude Hopkins, piano; Wendell Marshall, bass; Osie Johnson, drums.

"What Is This Thing Called Love?" "Empty Bed Blues," "Willow Weep for Me," "Yes, Indeed!" "It Don't Mean a Thing," "Morning Glory," "Is It So?" (Swingville SVLP2009).

Jimmy Rushing, *The Smith Girls*

Buck Clayton, trumpet; Dickie Wells and Benny Morton, trombones; Buster Bailey, clarinet; Claude Hopkins, piano; Everett Barksdale, guitar; Gene Raimey, bass; Jimmy Crawford, drums.

"Shipwrecked Blues," "Muddy Water," "Gulf Coast Blues," "Everybody Loves My Baby," "Trouble in Mind," "Downhearted Blues," "Squeeze Me," "How Come You Do Me Like You Do?" "Crazy Baby," "Arkansas Blues" (Col CL 1605).

Let's Jam

New York, February 21, 1961

Joe Thomas, trumpet; Buddy Tate, tenor and clarinet; Claude Hopkins, piano; Wendell Marshall, bass; J. C. Heard, drums.

"Safari Stomp," "Late Evening," "The Way You Look Tonight," "I Surrender Dear," "I Would Do Anything for You," "Off Beat Blues," "I Apologize" (Swingville SVLP 2020).

Swing Time

Bobby Johnson, trumpet; Vic Dickenson, trombone; Bud Johnson, tenor; Claude Hopkins, piano; Wendell Marshall, bass; Ferdinand Everett, drums.

"I Would Do Anything for You," "Somebody Love Me," "Stormy Weather," "Crying My Heart Out for You," "Love Me or Leave Me," "Mitzi," "On the Sunny Side of the Street" (Swingville SVLP 2041).

Introducing Cap'n John Handy

November 15–18, 1966

Doc Cheatham, trumpet; Benny Morton, trombone; Scoville Brown, clarinet, tenor; John Handy, alto; Claude Hopkins, piano; Eddie Gibbs, bass; Gus Johnson, drums.

"While We Danced at the Mardi Gras," "Bourbon St. Strut," "I Would Do Anything for You," "Baby, Won't You Please Come Home," "Handy's

Gulf Coast Boogie," "Cabaret," "Pass the Ribs," "One O'Clock Jump,"
"Perdido," "Good Feeling Blues," "I Laughed at Love" (RCA-Victor
LPM 3762).

Jazz Giants

Toronto, Canada, March 27–29, 1968

Claude Hopkins, piano; Wild Bill Davison, cornet; Herb Hall, clarinet;
Benny Morton, trombone; Arvell Shaw, bass; Buzzy Drootin, drums.

"Struttin' with Some Barbecue," "Dardenella [sic]," "Black and Blue," "I
Would Do Anything for You," "I've Found a New Baby," "Blue Again,"
"I Surrender Dear," "Yesterdays," "Them There Eyes" (Biograph BLP
3002, Sackville 3002).

Old Tyme Modern

Toronto, Canada, January 13, 1969

Herb Hall, clarinet; Arvell Shaw, bass; Buzzy Drootin, drums; Claude
Hopkins, piano.

"Old Fashioned Love," "All of Me," "Buddy Bolden's Blues," "Crying My
Heart Out for You," "Swingin' Down Shaw's Hall," "Beale St. Blues,"
"How Come You Do Me Like You Do?" "Willow Weep for Me," "Do
You Know What It Means to Miss New Orleans?" "Sweet Georgia Brown"
(Sackville 3003).

Solo Piano

New York, March 11, 1969

Claude Hopkins plays two tracks.

"57th St. Blues," "I Would Do Anything for You" (Swaggie S1387).

New York, March 26, 1969

Claude Hopkins plays two tracks.

"57th St. Blues," "I Got Rhythm" (Swaggie S1387).

Piano Jazz Masters

New York, early 1972

Claude Hopkins, solo piano.

"Three Little Words," "Squeeze Me," "Indiana" (Chiaroscuro CR170).

Sililoquy [*sic*]

Canada, May 13, 1972

Claude Hopkins, solo piano.

"Indiana," "Sugar," "If I Could Be with You," "Crazy Fingers," "You Took Advantage of Me," "Late Evening Blues," Safari Stomp," "New Orleans," "You're Driving Me Crazy," "Memphis Blues," "Who's Sorry Now?" (Sackville 3004).

Crazy Fingers

New York, 1973

Claude Hopkins, solo piano.

"Safari Stomp," "Blame It on a Dream," "I Would Do Anything for You," "58th [*sic*] Street Blues," "Willow Weep for Me," "Indiana," "Three Little Words," "Crying My Heart Out for You," "Low Gravy," "Crazy Fingers," "Late Evening Blues," "Hopkins's Scream" (Chiaroscuro 114).

Black & Blue

Valaurisis, France, July 17, 1974

Claude Hopkins, piano; Arvell Shaw, bass; Jo Jones, drums.

"I Would Do Anything for You," "Crying My Heart Out for You," "Struttin' with Some Barbecue," "Nice Blues," "Them There Eyes," "Poor Butterfly," "Safari Stomp," "I'm Coming Virginia," "I Got It Bad."

Sophisticated Swing

Manassas, Virginia, December 7–8, 1974

Recorded live at the Manassas Jazz Festival. Claude Hopkins plays piano on all tracks; Tom Saunders, cornet; Tommy Gwaltney, clarinet; Bill Allred, trombone; Butch Hall, guitar; Bill Goodall, bass; Ken Underwood, drums (Fat Cat's Jazz FCJ 197).

"Nobody's Sweetheart," "Yellow Dog Blues," "Deed I Do," "Sister Kate," "I Would Do Anything for You."

As above, except Gene Mayl, drums, replaced Goodall; Bill Barnes, trumpet, replaced Saunders; Bob Thompson, drums, replaced Underwood; Natalie Lamb, vocals; no guitar.

"Evil Hearted Woman"

As above, but Wild Bill Davison, trumpet, replaced Barnes; Nick Sassone, clarinet, replaced Gwaltney.

"Got Me Goin' "

Stan McDonald, soprano sax; Wild Bill Whelan, bass; Monty Mountjoy, drums.

"Blues My Naughty Sweetie Gives to Me"

As above, except McDonald switched to clarinet. Tony Pringle, cornet; Stan Vincent, trombone; and Peter Bullis, banjo, were added.

"Weary Blues"

Bibliography

Carr, Ian, Digby Fairweather, and Brian Priestly. *Jazz: The Essential Companion*. London: Grafton Books, 1987.

Chilton, John. *Who's Who of Jazz*. Philadelphia: Chilton Book Co., 1972; Time-Life Records Special Edition, 1979.

Clayton Peter, and Peter Gammond. *The Guinness Jazz A–Z*. Middlesex, England: Guinness Superlatives, 1986.

Dance, Stanley. *The World of Swing*. New York: Charles Scribners, 1974.

Gordon, Nightingale. *WNEW: Where the Melody Lingers On*. New York: Nightingale Gordon, 1984.

Kernfeld, Barry, ed. *New Grove's Dictionary of Jazz*. London: Macmillan Press, 1988.

Kinkle, Roger D. *The Complete Encyclopedia of Popular Music and Jazz: 1900–1950*. New Rochelle, N.Y.: Arlington House, 1974.

Meeker, David. *Jazz in the Movies*. New Rochelle, N.Y.: Arlington House, 1977.

Rust, Brian. *Jazz Records: 1897–1942*. New Rochelle, N.Y.: Arlington House, 1978.

Schuller, Gunther. *The Swing Era*. New York: Oxford University Press, 1989.

Selchow, Manfred. *Profoundly Blue: A Bio-Discographical Scrapbook on Edmond Hall*. West Germany: Selchow, 1988.

Simon, George T. *The Big Bands*. New York: Macmillan, 1967.

Ulanov, Barry. *Duke Ellington*. Reprint. New York: DaCapo Press, 1975.

Vaché, Warren W., Sr. *This Horn for Hire: The Life and Career of Pee Wee Erwin*. Metuchen, New Jersey: Scarecrow Press and the Institute of Jazz Studies, Rutgers University, 1987.

Index